Performance Management

Contents

Jeff Coates

Performance Management

The Chartered Institute of
Management Accountants

CIMA

Publishing

Copyright © CIMA 1997

First published in 1997 by:

The Chartered Institute of Management Accountants

63 Portland Place

London

W1N 4AB

ISBN 1 874784 76 0

Performance Management

Preface

Performance management in one sense encompasses all management activity in a business organisation, and as such would be well beyond the scope of a short book of this nature. The focus here is a narrower one: the creation of a unified system through which performance objectives may be established, how their degree of achievement may be measured and reported, and how managers together with other employees may be motivated towards attaining the desired results. The book is not prescriptive in presenting a formula for the content of such a system and how it should be made to function, since organisations will need to have regard to their own individual requirements.

Following the introductory Chapter 1, which emphasises the need for a performance management system, the main themes of this book are the creation of mission statements and objectives (Chapter 2), the measurement of performance (Chapters 3 and 4), motivation and reward (Chapter 4) and the communication of information (Chapter 5). Although treated as discrete topics, the creation and management of missions and objectives, performance measures and reward systems are clearly interdependent and interactive; they will be influenced by communication systems such as reporting mechanisms, as well as by other factors which lie outside the scope of this book, such as strategy development and resource allocation.

In order to reduce continual repetition of certain words, 'organisation' and 'company' are often used interchangeably as are 'performance indicators' and 'performance measures', though some commentators suggest that 'indicator' conveys a sense of looking forward, while 'measure' quantifies the outcome. Given that this book deals in general principles, no specific attempt is made to differentiate particular requirements, for example, for non-profit from profit-making organisations.

Chapter 1

The Need for a Performance Management System

INTRODUCTION

With the many references in the media and company reports to matters such as shareholder value maximisation, the interests of stakeholders in the economy, companies and other organisations and corporate governance, the question of performance and performance management is clearly of considerable interest today. The subject, however, is not exactly new: organisations have long been involved in planning and evaluating their performance through measuring financial returns, setting standards for performance and comparing budgetary outcomes with plans.

A major criticism of past performance management is that has been a fragmented activity, lacking in focus and cohesiveness, driven by a set of inappropriate and probably (in the view of some writers) incomplete objectives. Much of today's discussion of the topic therefore concentrates on the *concept* of a performance management system, which is comprehensive in embracing an organisation from the top to its lowest levels, is logically coherent and integral to its management as a whole.

Nevertheless, apart from the general outline of such systems, their exact structure and content and the way they are managed will be unique to individual organisations, dependent, for example, on the characteristics of the industries they belong to. Further, controversy continues to surround the use of certain performance measures, particularly financial ones. For these reasons, a universally acceptable blueprint scheme does not exist: each organisation must think through its own requirements; the literature may assist it in doing so, but does not provide the final solution.

The following extract from a CMA guideline (1994) provides the rationale for the renewed interest in performance management.

DEVELOPING COMPREHENSIVE PERFORMANCE INDICATORS
Society of Management Accountants of Canada, Management Accounting Guideline
31, *Developing Comprehensive Performance Indicators*, 1994

As industries and firms approach the twenty-first century, they are being confronted by business environments markedly different from those of the past. As customers have become increasingly educated and understand their requirements better, their expectations have increased. Competitors are becoming stronger and global in their perspective. Technological, social, regulatory, and other types of changes are, in many cases, accelerating.

To be successful in this new environment of the three C's – customers, competitors, and change – firms must adapt to the changing needs of customers better than their competitors along such dimensions as quality, speed, flexibility, variety and value. They must employ their resources, including investments in new product development, capital expenditures and people, productively. Ultimately, to increase shareholder value a firm must yield a return to its shareholders in excess of its cost of capital.

A number of firms have begun to manage themselves differently – focusing more explicitly on their customers, thinking and organising 'horizontally' rather than 'vertically,' emphasising cross-functional teams, and introducing new management techniques, such as business process analysis and activity-based costing.

Unfortunately, many firms' performance measurement systems have not been sufficiently redesigned to meet the needs of today's environment. Many systems primarily focus on measuring historical performance of internal operations, expressed in financial terms, using as a basis of measurement a set of budgeted figures against which actual results are compared. Measures are also very detailed, running the risk of local optimisation at the expense of what might be best for the firm as a whole. It has been said that 'you can't really understand a tennis match by just watching the score-board'. These traditional measurement systems must be expanded to deal with the future as well as the past, with external relationships and events as well as internal activities, and with non-financial as well as financial measures.

Proponents of the philosophy of total quality management (TQM) argue that focusing on leading indicators (such as market penetration, customer satisfaction, quality, speed, worker competence and morale) leads to good numbers; managing the numbers directly may mortgage the future. In addition to the traditional, historical, internal financial measures that give the 'score', performance measurement systems must focus on the future, on external relationships, and on non-financial as well as financial measures.

In an era of demanding markets and customers, strong competitors and rapid change, getting signals in advance of events lets the firm adjust and take corrective action before actual financial results have been realised.

Miskin's article both supports the CMA arguments and takes some points to geater depth.

PERFORMANCE MANAGEMENT
Andrew Miskin, *Management Accounting*, November 1995

Why do companies typically measure only about one-third of the things which are critical to their success in meeting their strategic business objectives? It is usually for one of three reasons:

- measurement systems are dominated by the demands of financial reporting. This inevitably puts too much focus on historical financial performance and can often only provide information to 'shut the stable door after the horse has bolted';
- measurement has usually evolved over a number of years. The pace of change in business markets has radically altered the business environment, and old measurement systems have not kept up and are no longer telling us what we now need to know;
- informal understanding of 'soft' issues (such as customer satisfaction or problem resolution) is relied upon; this was satisfactory in times of stability of purpose and personnel but is unreliable nowadays.

All of these are at best poor excuses and at worst dangerous signals for doing nothing now!

A core principle of management accounting is that the most reliable decisions are made based on facts. Organisations need to understand how well they are making progress towards all of their strategic goals. Traditional information has been largely based on historical financial performance; this is only one aspect of managing strategic performance. The performance of the business must be monitored over all aspects which are critical to its success, be they financial, operational or environmental. If an issue is vital then it needs to be measured, even if finding ways of measuring it are hard.

It is also important that measurement be directed to help to influence and forecast future performance rather than merely to understand and record past results. Measurements will need to be both financial and non-financial in nature and must be balanced to ensure that one objective is not pursued to the detriment of others. The philosophy should be to simplify information and focus management attention on those things which really matter to their business.

Performance measurement can only help the business if it is integrated with the management practices and control cycles of the organisation. There is a very close relationship between measurement and strategic thinking and planning; measurements must be compared with this strategic plan and not merely with budgets. Benefits can be realised by improving the quality of management decisions and by communicating with the staff what it is important for the organisation to achieve, thereby stimulating the organisation into continuous improvement.

If no coherent, consistent and interlocking set of strategic, process and operational measurements exists, it will be very hard for managers to set useful targets and standards for their employees.

Having the right measurements is vital since the very act of measurement affects behaviour. It is dangerous only to use measurements because they are available, concrete and understandable. If they are not carefully aligned with the strategic, operational and process objectives of the business, they will prompt behaviour which will run counter to these goals. It is also possible that areas which are not easily measured are ignored even though they are of vital importance.

Put simply, the way you reward and recognise your staff affects the way in which they behave.

Why, then, is there frequently little relationship between a demonstrable contribution to corporate goals and the individual's reward in most companies?

Many large companies have evolved hierarchical career ladders with reward and recognition coming largely through promotion. The various levels or grades have usually had inflexible salary bands attached to them.

This, of course, has controlled the overall salary bill and has had the merit of being relatively simple to administer and understand.

However, promotion has often had more to do with the political skills or time served by an employee, rather than demonstrable contribution towards overall organisational goals. Promotion usually acts like a ratchet – once someone has reached a certain level it is hard to reduce their reward regardless of their current contribution. For these reasons there is also little correlation between the pay and market worth of a member of staff.

The need to cut costs and to make organisations more efficient has led to the elimination of layers of management. This has drastically reduced the ability to use the promotional ladder as a reward mechanism and has made it more important to align all of the efforts of the staff to achieving the corporate objectives.

Companies are increasingly seeing the need to develop 'performance cultures', where it is contribution to corporate goals that is rewarded and not political skill, level or age. A performance culture:

- has defined clear, realistic corporate goals;
- has set local unit and individual goals which are congruent with the corporate goals;

- has communicated these goals, and they have been understood;
- positively reinforces the performance of individuals and teams in achieving their goals;
- is able to differentiate between levels of achievement.

To achieve this performance culture requires coherent direction-setting and performance measurement with aligned reward and recognition support systems.

To develop a performance culture it is vital to understand what constitutes a good performance. Merely doing what the boss says is not good enough. Of course, there will always need to be an element of managerial judgement in assessing the contribution of an individual, but a coherent and equitable set of measurable objectives forms a vital element in exercising this judgement.

There is a wide range of individual actions which is needed to support the business processes that meet the customer's needs and contribute to the success of overall strategic objectives. These actions need to be identified, and targets for achievement set for the key areas.

It is very important to remember that the setting of individual targets affects behaviour; indeed, that is their function. It is therefore vital to ensure that targets are set which stimulate the behaviour which contributes to business performance. For example, if sales targets alone are given to individuals, this may result in their ignoring vital aspects of customer service, or even trying to 'poach' sales from their colleagues. If inappropriate or unbalanced objectives are set, the wrong behaviour will result.

According to the CMA Guideline (1994), there is an active role for the management accountant to play in the creation of what it terms a new 'performance indicator system' (distinguishing 'indicators' from 'measures' broadly on the basis that the former are chosen to be forward-looking while the latter are more historical in nature):

- identifying the need for enhanced performance indicators;
- educating others about that need;
- developing a plan to identify the new performance indicators;
- predicting the behavioural impact of the new or revised performance indicators;
- developing a plan for implementing the new system, including its underlying architecture;
- implementing the new process; and
- assessing the new performance indicator's effect on the organisation and continually improving upon that indicator.

Altogether this assumes a high degree of involvement, though needless to say within the formats that senior management will lay down: the management accountant can probably at best advise. Lothian (1987) identifies one factor as having a major influence on the shape of management accounting practice then, which remains a part of the controversy surrounding performance measurement today, namely 'the capital market's obsession with bottom-line profit as almost the sole indicator of corporate performance'. This he suggests

encourages management to take a number of actions which focus on the short term at the expense of investing for the long-term survival and growth of their organisations. One such action is the cutting back of R&D expenditure in an effort to minimise the impact on the costs side of the current year's profit and loss account. A related impact of the obsession with annual profit is that managers seek information on profits at more frequent intervals, sometimes as often as weekly, to ensure that they will be on target with market expectation at the end of the year; external reporting mechanisms, in other words, are used by many organisations as ongoing management control reports, a role for which they were not designed.

Although 'bottom-line' profit in the absolute sense may no longer always be the single measure of success or otherwise, it is commonly used in conjunction with other measures and forms a part of such others as earnings per share and return on capital employed. As a result, similar criticism to the above may be directed at the latter, not to mention the existence of factors such as the historical nature of the data and its roots in accounting method. The 'capital market' (a very broad entity) by no means fully accepts this criticism; this had led to an extensive and, so far, largely inconclusive debate as to responsibility for the causes and consequences of perceived short-termism and what should be done to overcome it.

A useful summary for a positive approach to performance management comes from Fitzgerald and Moon (1996). Their research led them to consider the following 'five common characteristics' to represent best practice:

- Know what you are trying to do – this must be driven by corporate strategy;
- Adopt a range of measures – financial and non-financial;
- Extract comparative measures – there must be a benchmark for performance;
- Report results regularly – this discipline promotes knowledge and action;
- Drive the system from the top – senior management need to use the system.

As noted at the outset, the profile of performance management has been considerably raised in recent years. However, to avoid the impression that it represents something entirely new, superseding all that has gone before, it may be as well to remember that it is related in many ways to budgetary planning and control. Setting standards and measuring departures therefrom are a central part of performance evaluation in budgetary planning and control. The contribution of a new performance management system is likely to be a much widened perspective of an organisation's business, focusing on its external environment as well as internal operations and taking a balanced approach to the establishment of objectives, targets and measures. Questions surrounding the issues of motivation, reward, communication and reporting, often collectively referred to as behavioural aspects of management accounting, have also long been linked to budgetary planning and control. The concepts and principles pertaining to these aspects, however, undergo little, if any, change, when viewed in the context of a performance management system. Consequently, they receive less attention in this book than does the creation of a performance measurement/indicator system.

An extract from Dugdale (in Chapter 3) supports the view that behavioural factors are an accepted feature of budgetary planning. It is included here to emphasise the continuity element in the development of performance management systems.

BUDGETS AND THEIR BEHAVIOURAL CONSEQUENCES

If you have been involved in the preparation and use of budgets you will realise that it is not quite the straightforward technical analysis which introductory textbooks portray. Partly the complexities can be attributed to the multiple uses of budgets:

- planning
- communicating — the plans of top management down the line;
- co-ordinating — the efforts of marketing, production, development,
- authorising — expenditure by managers;
- controlling — by comparing actual results with budget and requiring action to regain control when necessary;
- motivating — by setting a target for managers to aim for;
- evaluating — the performance of managers.

These multiple uses of budgets usually lead to a number of tensions within the organisation. For example:

- for planning, a budget should be realistic, as overoptimistic sales projections or cost targets will lead to problems with profit and cash flow;
- but, for motivation, arguably a budget should be 'tight', setting challenging targets which will motivate managers and workers to try harder – although the targets might not actually be met;
- for evaluation, higher management may desire a 'tight but achievable' budget while those being evaluated will naturally want a slack budget which will allow an apparently high performance.

There have been many studies of budgeting systems, with some of the classic work being carried out in the 1950s and 1960s. One of the earliest and most quoted works is that by Argyris, *The Impact of Budgets on People*. Argyris draws attention to the manner in which budgets can be employed as 'pressure devices' and the way in which organisational conflict can be generated. A budget can provide a convenient 'scapegoat' for management to use when they wish to exert pressure.

SUMMARY

As the CMA Guideline quoted at the outset suggests, todays' organisations must address a wide range of potential objectives, beyond the familiar financial ones. It is contended that, in the past, the majority of performance management systems have been limited in outlook and unsystematic in application. A more comprehensive and cohesive system is now necessary, though this will need to be designed to meet the unique demands of managing individual organisations.

Commencing with the mission and objectives of an organisation, subsequent chapters present and discuss the principal features of a broadly based, co-ordinated system

REFERENCES

- Argyris, C (1952), *The Impact of Budgets on People*, Controllership Foundation, New York, Ithaca
- Fitzgerald, L and Moon, P (1996) *Performance Measurement in Service Industries: Making it Work*, CIMA Publishing.
- Lothian, N (1987) *Measuring Corporate Performance*, CIMA Publishing.

Chapter 2

Mission and Corporate Objectives

INTRODUCTION

It is necessary for an organisation to formulate its mission, goals and objectives, and in this it is important to distinguish between these concepts.

Mintzberg (1983) provides definitions as follows:

1. *Mission:* An organisation's mission is its basic function in society and is reflected in the products and services that it provides for its customers or clients. For example, although all publishers are in the business of publishing and selling books to readers, there is within this industry a great variety of missions which publishers follow. Thus, the UK publishing house Virago has a fundamental mission, which is the dissemination of 'women's views on life through the publication of books by women for women'. Consequently books selected by Virago for publishing are based on their currency as well-written literary vehicles of 'women's views' rather than their market potential. This is a somewhat different mission than that followed by the publishers of cheap, mass-market paperback books. Thus the mission of an organisation is essentially a long-term – many years – view of its fundamental reasons for existence.

2. *Goals:* An organisation's goals are the intentions behind its decisions or actions. Goals will frequently never be achieved and may be incapable of being measured. Thus, for example, the United Biscuits goal of giving 'the highest possible standard of living to our employees' is a goal which will be difficult to realise and measure. Therefore, although goals are more specific than a mission statement and tend to have a shorter number of years in their time scales, they are not precise measures of performance.

3. *Objectives:* Objectives are goals expressed in a form in which they can be measured. Thus, the objective of 'profit before interest and tax to be not less than 20 per cent of capital employed' – is capable of precise measurement.

AN ORGANISATION'S MISSION

'MISSION' AND STRATEGIC PLANNING
Steven Braund, *CIMA Student*, February 1991

What is mission?

The CIMA definition of strategy indicates that since strategic planning depends on objectives or targets, the obvious starting point for a study of strategic planning is the identification and formulation of objectives.

Although discussion of organisational objectives often subsumes mission, most management or corporate strategy texts distinguish between the two. Mintzberg (1983), for example, refers to objectives as the *intentions* of the organisation expressed in a form in which they can be measured and mission as the organisation's *basic function in society*.

The organisation's mission is its foundation stone, its underpinning which persists even when shorter-term objectives change. If for some reason the mission of the firm should change (e.g. change of ownership or management) then this will clearly affect both objectives and strategy.

Searching for a definition of mission can be frustrating: there are almost as many definitions of mission as there are authors on the subject. Moreover, the definitions are wide-ranging and ambiguous. Consider the following definitions of mission.

Richards (1978) adopts an almost rhetorical approach, defining mission as a: '... master strategy ... a visionary projection of the central and overriding concepts on which the organisation is based'.

A somewhat less grand but rather more manageable definition is provided by Thompson (1990): 'The essential purpose of the organisation, ... why it is in existence, the nature of the business(es) it is in, and the customers it seeks to serve and satisfy'.

Both definitions are typically general and lack detail (although the latter takes consideration of the organisation's context, what it does and in which market it operates). However, according to David (1986), this absence of detail is desirable for two reasons: first because it allows for greater scope and flexibility to develop alternative strategies and objectives and, second, because it allows for the satisfaction of the needs of the various groups of people which are involved with an organisation.

Thus it should come as no surprise that the mission statements of organisations lack the clarity and detail that one would expect to find in their stated objectives.

The importance of mission

Many authors believe that mission is of such fundamental importance to the organisation that it should constitute the first step in the strategic decision-making process. Among them is Peter Drucker (1989), one of the best-known and respected writers on management, who asserts that: 'Only a clear definition of the mission and purpose of the business makes possible clear and realistic business objectives. It is the foundation for priorities, strategies, plans and work assignments. It is the starting point for the design of managerial jobs....'

Others would contest the positioning of the determination of mission and objectives in the strategic planning process (see Figure 1, which is the typical model of that process), maintaining that this stage should come after the analysis of the environment in which the organisation operates. They would, however, agree that the organisation should attempt to set its objectives only after the formulation of the organisational mission (see Smith et al. (1988) and Wheelan and Hunger (1989)).

By contrast, Argenti (1989) finds the idea of deciding on a mission statement as the first (or even one of the first) and crucial step in the corporate-planning process 'ridiculous' and goes on to say: 'I am alarmed and astounded when textbooks suggest that they [mission statements] should *precede* [Argenti's emphasis] the corporate planning process, that companies should make their mission statements before they start their corporate plan.'

Figure 1: The strategic management model

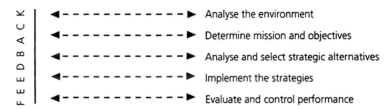

Source: Smith, Arnold and Bizzell: *Business Strategy and Policy*, Houghton Mifflin

Mission statements, he believes, should be outputs from, not the inputs to, the strategic planning process, developed through 'careful logical discussion'.

Other advocates of the importance of the role of mission to an organisation include Greenley (1989) who, like Drucker, believes mission is '... the logical starting point of strategic management ... as it affects the other stages of strategic management'. Greenley identified a number of reasons for establishing a corporate mission statement (Table 1).

Table 1: Reasons for organisational mission

1	Unanimity of purpose
2	Resource utilisation
3	Company climate and philosophy
4	Long-range vision
5	Business domain specification
6	Market-base orientation
7	Motivation of personnel

'Company climate and philosophy' (number 3 in Table 1), for example, will regulate the behaviour of the individuals who make up the organisation through an organisational mission statement which 'epitomises the values, beliefs and guidelines' that comprise the business culture. 'Motivation of personnel' (number 7 in Table 1) can be achieved if the mission statement is 'able to encompass the nature of the company's business in a format which is readily available to and is easily understood by personnel'.

Personnel should be able to 'understand the direction in which the company is going, as well as the way in which their roles relate to this overall direction'.

Few would dispute the worthiness of the reasons listed in Table 1, but it is apparent that some difficulty must be encountered when attempting to encapsulate the sentiment behind them in one brief statement.

Smith et al. (*ibid.*) point out that all components of the mission may not be included in the publicised mission statement and that some organisations may have 'unwritten mission(s)'. However, this would seem to raise an additional problem of how stakeholders (personnel, for example) gain access to the parts of the statement which refer to them so that they may understand and participate in the fulfilment of the mission as Greenley envisages and, presumably, the organisation desires.

Pearce and Robinson (1985) offer a list of criteria that mission statements should incorporate (Table 2), most of which appear to be reasonable (i.e. helping to establish or outline the organisation's 'basic purpose in society'). 'Growth and profitability' (number 4 in Table 2), which might have looked more comfortable in a list of objectives, is included 'to give direction on the general rate of growth and the ultimate size seen to be valid for the future' rather than to specify particular targets for growth and profitability.

Table 2: Criteria to be included in the mission

1 Basic product/service definition
2 Definition of customers and markets
3 Technology
4 Growth and profitability
5 Company philosophy
6 Social responsibility and public image

Examples of 'mission' statements

The following examples of mission statements are taken from well-known and successful business organisations. They range:

from the easily understood:

> 'Quality food products; efficient, friendly service; and restaurants renowned for the cleanliness and value they provide' (McDonald's Corporation);

to the apparently flippant:

> 'What is our mission statement? It's easy – we will be the most honest cosmetic company around. How will we do it? That's easy too – we will go diametrically in the opposite direction to the cosmetic industry' (Anita Roddick, Body Shop);

to the Utopian:

> 'The supreme purpose of the whole organisation is to secure the fairest possible sharing by all the members [the firm's term for its employees] of all the advantages of ownership – gain, knowledge and power. That is to say, their happiness in the broadest sense of that word, so far as happiness depends upon gainful occupation' (John Lewis Partnership).

Each of these mission statements is very different from the others. This is to be expected as they are operating in different markets and have different histories, types of workforce, culture, etc. Despite these significant differences it is clear that they are not formulated in strict accordance with the guidance provided above unless, of course, these public statements of organisational mission have been edited (see Smith et al.(*ibid*)). The Body Shop mission statement, in particular, reads like a remark made during an interview; more an indictment of the cosmetics industry than a well thought-through statement of the principles underlying Body Shop's operations.

This may be entirely intentional. Argenti (*ibid*), who we have seen is critical of the textbook approach to mission statements, nevertheless believes that they can be very useful as long as they are seen for what they are. He says: 'I believe that mission statements are nothing to do with corporate planning, they are public relations statements.' Thus mission statements become public relations tools, something that the public and all groups associated with the organisation can identify with, a rallying cry for those whom Argenti refers to as 'troops'. Moreover, in the case of the Body Shop mission statement it is quite likely that Argenti would not deem this a mission statement at all but merely a statement of corporate conduct, a description of how the company intends to behave itself in society rather than what it is for.

Summary

Mission, it seems, is essentially a conception of the purpose of the organisation, an open-ended non-specific statement of the reason for the organisation's existence. There is little agreement on what the mission statement should look like, although some authors have attempted to establish criteria. There is the suspicion on the part of some writers, most notably Argenti, that an organisation's mission is merely a publicity or motivational device.

Two complete mission statement examples are quoted below:

- **From the 1996 Annual Report and Accounts of BT Plc:**
  'BT's mission, our central purpose, is to provide world-class telecommunications and information products and services, and to develop and exploit our networks, at home and overseas, so that we can: meet the requirements of our customers, sustain growth in the earnings of the group on behalf of our shareholders, and make a fitting contribution to the community in which we conduct our business.'

- **From the 1996/97 Annual Report of BAA Plc:**
  'Our mission is to make BAA the most successful airport company in the world.
    This means:
    → Always focusing on our customers' needs and safety.
    → Achieving continuous improvements in the costs and quality of our processes and services.
    → Enabling our employees to give of their best.

To achieve our mission we will:

Safety and security
Give safety and security the highest priority at all times by systematically assessing and managing our safety and security risks through audited, best practice management systems.

Employees
Provide a good and safe working environment which attracts and retains committed employees. Through training and two-way communication allow them to fulfil their potential and contribute directly to the success of the company

Customers, suppliers and business partners
Ensure our passengers and airlines receive excellence and good value for money in the services BAA provides and work together with our suppliers and business partners to create added value for all concerned.

Strategy
Concentrate on the core airport business, be prudently financed, continuously improve quality and cost effectiveness, become excellent in information technology, fully develop our property and retail potential, achieve world-class standards in capital investment and develop an international business which enhances the quality and growth prospects of the Group.

Shareholders
Encourage shareholders to believe in our company by giving them consistent growth in earnings and dividends.

Environment
Recognise the concerns of the local communities, set challenging environmental targets and audit our performance against them.'

There is some commonality of context between the two, with BAA being rather more comprehensive and definitive. Both appeared prominently at the front of the reports, though interestingly, the 1997 report of BT has dropped the statement in favour of one explaining the proposed BT–MCI merger. However, its Business Review could be said to expand on much of the one given in the previous year.

On the whole, mission statements have had a somewhat uneven reception, being regarded by some as mere motherhood expressions, while others appear to value their attempt to concisely signal an organisation's priorities.

Accepting the Mintzberg view of a rather blurred distinction existing between missions and goals, the latter will not be discussed further. Objectives, though, are seen as capable of measurement and hence are fundamental to the evaluation of performance at various levels throughout an organisation, as the following extract from Harvey makes clear.

STRATEGIC OBJECTIVES

THE CHARACTERISTICS OF STRATEGIC OBJECTIVES
Michael Harvey, *Strategic Management Accountancy and Marketing: Practical Elements*, CIMA 1994

An organisation must establish objectives if it is to measure how efficient the resource conversion process is in relation to achieving the objective. Objectives should be established at three levels: *primary* – that is corporate/strategy objectives which concern the company; *secondary* – that is tactical/managerial objectives which concern the strategic business unit; and those at the lowest level, the *operational/administrative* objectives which are related to units such as departments.

Objectives are likely to be based on a combination of purpose and ethos. The *purpose* element relates to why the organisation was formed; this usually means that its activities must be of benefit to shareholders: thus a major objective is likely to concern profit generation even if not to maximise shareholders' wealth. The *ethos* element concerns a concept similar to culture and so will interact with, and be developed within, the context of the history of the organisation and the environment within which it operates. Thus the ethos aspect of objectives will be influenced by such things as an organisation's history, traditions, ownership, size, approach to risk, what is produced, method of production, markets, its attitude towards society and society's attitudes towards it.

An organisation will establish overall strategic objectives which in private-sector organisations are likely to be related to such factors as: *profitability*, which may cover capital gearing, retained profits, taxation, dividends and inflation; financial and physical resources related to internal and external capital, the latter classified by its form and source (e.g. whether obtained through leasing, etc.); *production*, related to such things as research and development, design, productivity, quality and packaging ; *management*, covering performance, the organisation structure, the ability of the firm to recruit managers, their ability to communicate, quality, education and training, style and pecuniary rewards; *employees'* performance and attitude, which include their availability, training and development, quality, promotional opportunities, relationship with management and pecuniary rewards; *marketing*, including market standing, the products sold, services provided, market penetration, market position (i.e. share) and leadership (in pricing/innovation); and *corporate social responsibility*, which concerns such things as ethics, employee welfare, involvement in the local community, contribution towards environmental conservation and avoiding socially undesirable activities, and consumer protection.

In establishing objectives, remembering there may be multiple objectives for different factors and areas, although profitability must inevitably be one of the main ones, it is crucial to establish a balance between these other factors and the short- and long-term impact of these. A number of groups, today frequently referred to as stakeholders, will influence the objective that an organisation can establish. These include shareholders, investment analysts, debt holders, customers, suppliers, trade associations, trade unions, government (both central and local), society, company directors, managers, supervisors and the workforce generally.

The traditional objective of the firm, drawn from the economic model of the firm operating in a situation of perfect competition, is profit maximisation. To achieve maximum profits the business has to know something about marginal analysis, and this really requires the owner to manage the business. It should be noted that short-run profit maximisation may not lead to long-run profit maximisation. However, since the Industrial Revolution, there has generally been a divorce of ownership from control in all but the smallest of firms; institutional investors (pension funds, unit trusts, investment trusts, trade unions, insurance companies, etc.) have increasingly taken up equity and today have a great influence on corporate objectives.

Profit maximisation is based on the following assumptions: there are a large number of buyers and sellers in the market who act independently (i.e. there is no collusion); all products are homogeneous (i.e. exactly the same); all buyers and sellers have complete information about the market, and there are no barriers to entry into or exit from the industry. In the real world the entrepreneur will find it advantageous to break down these assumptions and gain a competitive advantage in so doing.

Today, the macro objectives of a firm include sales maximisation and growth and the development of such things as satisficing and the survival of the technostructure. It is important to balance an organisation's strategic objectives to enable it to achieve balanced growth and development.

John Argenti (1973), in 'Setting Objectives – A Practical Approach', discusses practical aspects associated with setting objectives. He points out that there is no general agreement as to what the long-term objectives of an organisation should be, though he provides examples of these and, in pursuing them, the questions they cause to be raised. However, he spends considerable time discussing the importance of growth. He explains that an organisation is likely to have a number of subsidiary objectives. He concludes by discussing the characteristics of meaningful objectives.

John Fawn (1987), in 'The History, Culture and Leadership of a Company', writes of the importance of leadership and culture to a company. He discusses Michael Porter's generic strategies of cost leadership, differentiation and focus and provides examples of these from real firms. He goes on to discuss when it may be necessary for an organisation to change its culture, and finally he looks at the position of the planner and company culture.

OBJECTIVES IN PRACTICE

A study of five large multinational companies in each of the UK, USA and Germany by Coates et al. (1993) reported a standard listing of objectives by type. In the following tables HO = Head Office; Sub = Subsidiary; O = Objective quoted.

Objectives – UK companies

Objectives emphasised (0)	UK1 HO	UK1 SUB	UK2 HO	UK2 SUB	UK3 HO	UK3 SUB	UK4 HO	UK4 SUB	UK5 HO	UK5 SUB
General										
Profitability	O[1]	O	O	O	O[3]	O[3]	O[4]	O	O[5]	O
Growth/market share		O		O				O	O[5]	O
Cash flow/liquidity		O	O	O		O	O	O		O
Financial stability		O			O		O			
Productivity						O				
Employee welfare/safety										
Environmental										
Max. shareholder wealth			O[2]							

[1] NPV of future cash flows

[2] share price growth

[3] EPS, ROCE + gearing – in that order

[4] Real return on equity

[5] 1st = Bottom line + growth in sales

Objectives – US companies

Objectives emphasised (0)	US1 HO	US1 SUB	US2 HO	US2 SUB	US3 HO	US3 SUB	US4 HO	US4 SUB	US5 HO	US5 SUB
General					O					
Profitability	O[1]	O=	O	O=	O		O	O	O	O
Growth/market share	O=	O=	O	O=		O	O		O	O
Cash flow/liquidity		O=			O			O		
Financial stability							O		O	
Productivity						O				
Employee welfare/safety						O				
Environmental					O					

[1] EPS as surrogate for market value of stock

O = Equal weight given to each objective

Objectives – German companies

Objectives emphasised (0)	GR1 HO	GR1 SUB	GR2 HO	GR2 SUB	GR3 HO	GR3 SUB	GR4 HO	GR4 SUB	GR5 HO	GR5 SUB
General										
Profitability	O	O	O	O	O=	O=	O	O	O	O
Growth/market share	O			O	O=	O=		O		
Cash flow/liquidity										O
Financial stability									O	
Productivity	O								O	
Employee welfare/safety	O							O		
Environmental	O							O		

O = Equal weight given to each objective

The lists themselves contain few surprises, though in view of the content of the next chapter, it is notable that only one company (from the UK) directly quoted maximisation of shareholder wealth to be an objective. Otherwise profitability and growth/market share are the dominant objectives, with little commonality about the remainder. This underlines the impossibility of drawing up generalised schemes: individual organisations tailor them to their own situations. In addition, it was found there was no straightforward link between missions and objectives; German companies, for example, tended to stress marketing aspects to a greater extent in their mission statements than profitability (and consequently, returns to shareholders), though this does not imply a breakdown in logic.

In case readers may wonder, the companies were reluctant to provide quantified information and (unsurprisingly) would not discuss strategies aimed at achieving them.

SUMMARY

Many organisations, commercial and non-commercial, have adopted mission statements. Their purpose should be a succinct expression of an organisation's reason for being and the way it intends to conduct its affairs. The old maxim that a commercial business exists to make money is seen as over-simplistic; the mission generally reflects the need to meet the interests of a number of stakeholders. It provides a focus which should be easy to recall. Statements may also be tailored to meet the needs of individual sectors of an organisation.

If a mission is to have real meaning, its essence must be converted into a set of objectives, each contributing to its realisation in ways capable of measurement. Objectives will cascade down through an organisation from the strategic to the operational levels. They will need to be balanced overall and as to their impact on decision-making; for example, are they likely to result in a greater stress on achieving results in the short term rather than the long term?

The following chapter deals with the measures which may be adopted to monitor the achievement of objectives and briefly discusses their nature and limitations.

REFERENCES

- Argenti, J L (1989), *Practical Corporate Planning*, Unwin.
- Argenti, J L (1973), 'Setting Objectives – A Practical Approach', in Sadler, P and Robson, A (eds), *Corporate Planning and the Role of the Management Accountant*, ICMA and the Society for Long-range Planning.
- Coates, J B, Davis, E W, Longden, S G, Stacey, R J and Emmanuel, C (1993), *Corporate Performance Evaluation in Multinational Companies*, CIMA.
- David, F R (1986), *Fundamentals of Strategic Management*, Merrill.
- Drucker, P F (1989), *The Practice of Management*, Heinemann.
- Fawn, J (1987), 'The History, Culture and Leadership of a Company', in Fawn, J and Cox, B (eds), *Corporate Planning in Practice*, Kogan Page.
- Greenley, G (1989), *Strategic Management*, Prentice-Hall.
- Howe, W S (1986), *Corporate Strategy*, Macmillan, 1986.
- Mintzberg, H (1983), *Power In and Around Organisations*, Prentice-Hall.
- Pearce, J A and Robinson, R B (1985), *Strategic Management, Strategy Formulation and Implementation*, Irwin.
- Richards, M D (1978), *Organisational Goal Structures*, West.
- Smith, G D, Arnold D R and Bizzell, B G (1988), *Business Strategy and Policy*, Houghton Mifflin.

- Thompson, J L (1990), *Strategic Management Awareness and Change*, Chapman and Hall.
- Wheelan, T L and Hunger, J D (1989), *Strategic Management and Business Policy*, Addison-Wesley.

Chapter 3

Measuring Performance at Corporate and Business-sector Levels

INTRODUCTION

Clearly specified objectives will, for the most part, indicate the measures required to quantify their degree of achievement. For example, for an objective stated to be 'to achieve a 10 per cent increase in EPS', EPS is obviously the measure. This might not always be the case, however, for an objective may rather vaguely be stated to be 'to improve shareholder value' (though hopefully such expressions are mostly confined to mission statements).

In the previous chapter it was noted that companies may aim to achieve several objectives, but commonly (among commercial organisations) there will be an objective related to profitability. In the group of companies in the Coates study (see Chapter 2), the majority assigned a high priority to the achievement of 'profitability', but measured it in different ways. It is widely accepted that in the past (and the indications are that the same goes for the present) performance management at corporate and business levels has tended to rely heavily on historical financial measures of profitability such as EPS and ROI for guidance. However, as the CMA Guideline (1994) puts it: ' this ... will usually be inadequate in today's and tomorrow's business environment'.

This chapter briefly directs attention to the 'coherence' requirement of a performance management system and then discusses issues surrounding, in particular, the profitability measures of performance on the grounds that they remain prominent, if not always the pre-eminent, measures.

MEASUREMENT SYSTEMS

Figures 1 and 2 are extracted from the CMA Guideline (*ibid*). Figure 1 illustrates the links between (commercial) business operations, reported results and (in this case) the ultimate objective of shareholder value expressed as the NPV (net present value) of the future stream of cash flows). It makes clear that whatever sub-objectives/measures of performance may be introduced below this ultimate level, they should conform and contribute to attaining the latter: an ill-considered jumble of unrelated, maybe contradictory, measures is of no help. Figure 2 expresses the connections between planning and managing performance, again underlining the need to have a unified view of the system as a whole. It also incorporates links to the wider external business markets environment.

Relationships such as these have been presented in a variety of ways by other authors, for example Porter (1980, 1985), a feature of most being the inclusion of the external business environment in one way or another, emphasising the shift from purely inward looking systems.

In the next chapter, the concept of the balanced scorecard, originated by Kaplan and Norton (1992), will be discussed as a way of securing cohesiveness within a system.

Figure 1: Relationship between processes, decisions and results

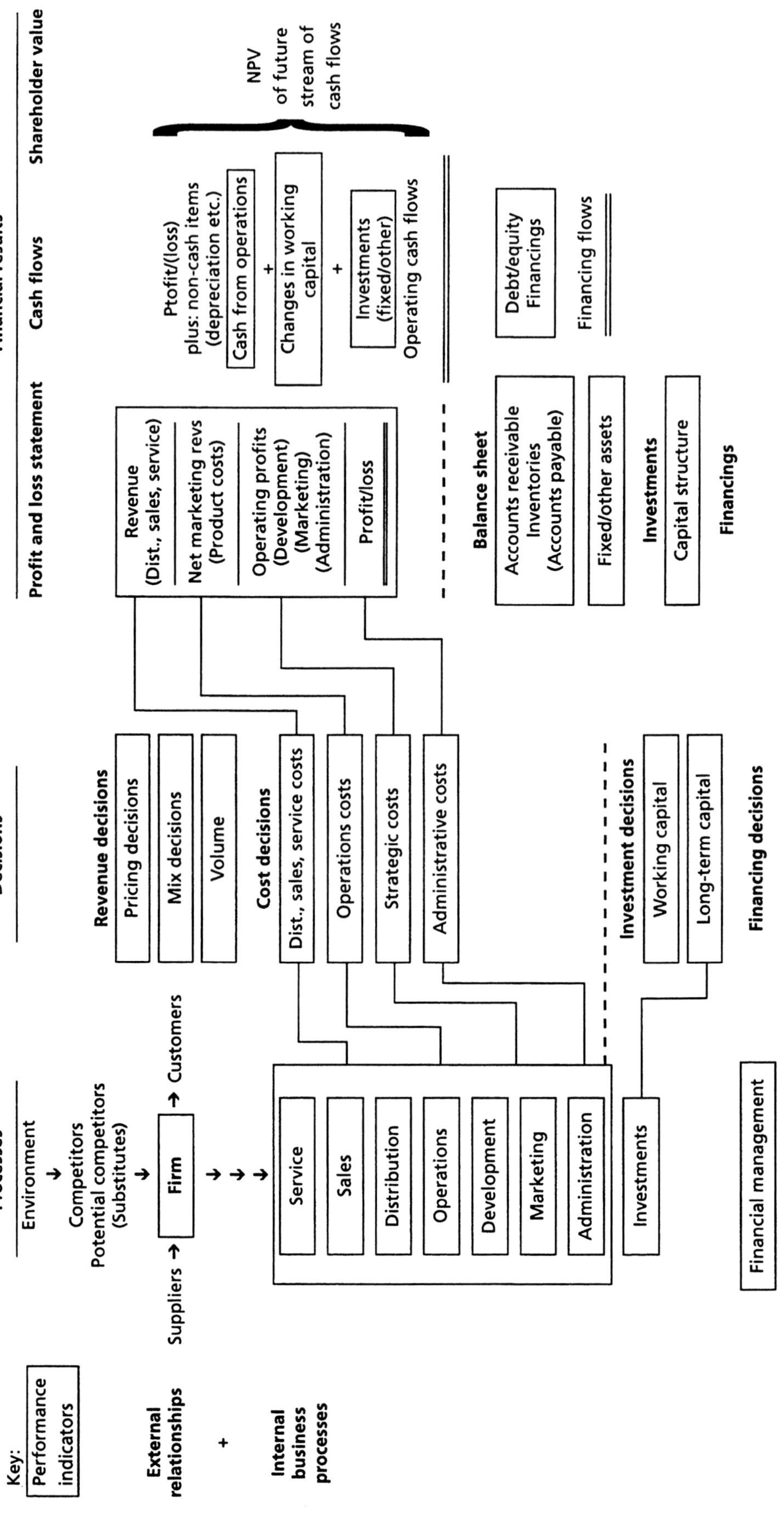

Figure 2: Managing/measuring the enterprise as a system

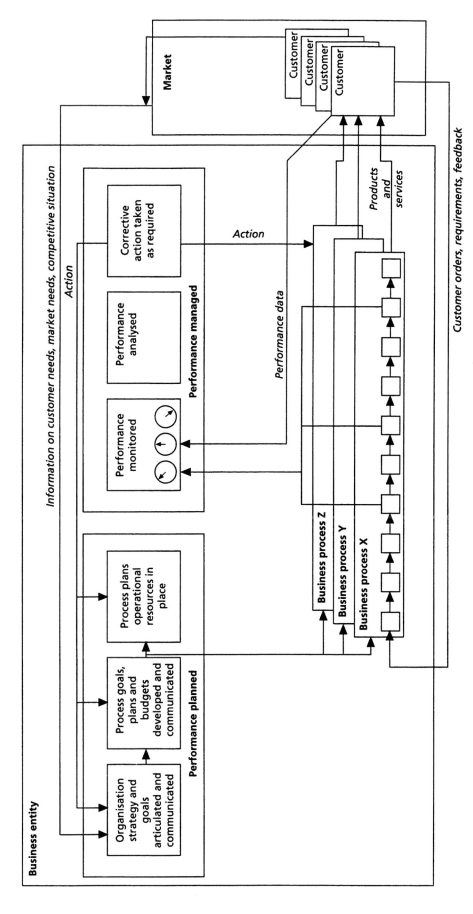

MEASURING CORPORATE PERFORMANCE

Figure 1 shows the generation of NPV to be the final goal/objective/measure of business performance. It is defined as the difference between the discounted value of a future cash-flow stream and the cost of the capital required to run the business. The latter should reflect the risk/uncertainty factor inherent in the nature of that business as well as the interest cost of money. A positive NPV represents an increase in shareholders' wealth/value, and this return is widely argued to be the most economically sound measure of business performance: not only may shareholders benefit, but a fund may be created to meet other, for example, environmental objectives, while maintaining a sound financial base. The extension of this principle from the corporate level to that of the business sector, though, may be problematic and more difficult to achieve.

Although apparently theoretically sound, NPV and its derivatives (to be introduced later) do not as yet appear to figure prominently among measures actually in use at either corporate- or business-sector levels: as noted earlier, it is traditional accounting measures which continue to hold sway.

This situation has given rise to a controversy which leaves the question of what is the best (financial) measure of corporate (and sector) performance unresolved. It is a controversy linked not only to the alternative measures themselves, but also to incentive reward schemes and issues surrounding the inducement to short-termist thinking among managers. A detailed exposition of these issues, which space precludes from entering into here, is given in Cornelius and Davies (1997), but Coates et al. (1996) provide a brief summary of some aspects in the following extract.

FINANCIAL MEASURES
J B Coates, E Davis, N Reeves and A Zafar, *Challenging Short-termism*, CIMA, 1996

In recent years there has been a growing body of literature from various sources criticising short-run accounting-based profit measures and their use, both in corporate performance measurement and in incentive reward schemes....

Accounting values of earnings and profitability such as earnings per share (EPS), return on investment (ROI), return on capital employed (ROCE), return on equity (ROE) and absolute profit (to quote the most commonly observed ones) are short run, i.e. quoted as annual, half-yearly or even quarterly figures. Their use in a corporate performance measurement system is considered to lend a short-run focus to management actions (Rappaport(1986); Ezzamel (1992); Ezzamel and Hart(1989)) to the exclusion of long-term performance measurement and, according to Rappaport, shareholder value. Bennett-Stewart is an author very critical of the use of EPS, suggesting that the assumption that what the market wants is 'earnings and wants them now', is one lacking 'any shred of convincing evidence' in support of it. This, of course, raises the issue of whether markets are truly short-termist, as popular belief suggests, an issue also examined by Marsh (1990). The use of the price/earnings (P/E) multiple for company valuation is also criticised by Bennett-Stewart (1991) for its 'utter lack of realism', commenting that its appeal is founded (misleadingly) on 'simplicity and apparent precision'.

The inherent deficiencies of accounting-based numbers is not confined to their short-run focus, but to other characteristics which could result in the lack of goal congruence. These are typically listed as:

- the use of accrual-based accounting methods, primarily designed for external reporting rather than future planning;
- they stress past rather than future performance;
- capital values are accounting book values;

- application of different accounting methods, e.g. with respect to inventory valuation, produces different results, whether or not deliberate manipulation is involved;
- economic risk is not in general explicitly recognised where reference is made to some hurdle cost of capital criterion, such as is the case in the residual income measure and could be the case for return on investment (ROI) and return on capital employed (ROCE); even if it were, judging the acceptability of accounting returns against economic opportunity cost is not comparing like with like;
- they are not necessarily consistent with the creation of value for shareholders.

As Rappaport (1986, Ch. 2) observed: 'In both corporate reports and the financial press, there is an obsessive fixation on earnings per share (EPS) as the scorecard of corporate performance.' It is commonly assumed that if a company produces 'satisfactory' growth in EPS, then the market value of its shares will increase. Rappaport then goes on to make a crucial observation that 'EPS growth does not necessarily lead to an increase in the market value of stock.'

Given the popularity of share option schemes as an incentive for (usually) senior managers, the 'spur from the financial markets' cannot readily be disassociated from the scheme of performance measures which these senior managers will have approved. EPS is certainly a widely adopted performance measure, as well as being an almost universally quoted statistic in UK company reports In particular, with respect to EPS, several writers (Bennett-Stewart (1991), Kay (1991), Barfield (1994)) stress that:

- (as Rappaport) there is only a limited relationship between EPS and the creation of value by a company;
- EPS may be shown to grow simply by achieving a return greater than the interest in borrowed money, thus leading to investment which may actually destroy value for shareholders. Risk normally means that returns to shares are much higher than pure interest costs;
- EPS does not take into account the amount of cash needed to acquire fixed assets, extra working capital and acquisitions;
- as an accounting measure, there can be substantial differences between companies and time periods as accounting treatments change (though FRS3 in the UK has tightened up on this).

Two other issues arise in relation to the use of EPS as a performance measure: first, the belief that a good record on EPS growth will enhance share price and hence reward a (mainly senior) management, incentivised by share option schemes, and second, whether senior management's commitment to such a share price maximisation strategy is further undermined by the use of defective measures, for example, ROCE, in pursuit of the EPS outcome.

Although accounting measures such as ROI come in for severe criticism from many quarters, it is worth noting that not all would agree. Particularly in the context of divisional management it is claimed that use of, e.g. ROI/ROCE, as principal financial performance measures leads managers to aim to increase revenues, reduce costs and keep capital employed to a minimum in order to produce high returns. This is obviously desirable within the framework of an organisation's overall objectives, but the problems really tend to lie with how the measures are compiled and the resultant signals they provide as to the best course of action to take.

Its is probable that growth in earnings per share continues to dominate the way senior management (as well as many others) perceive their success or otherwise in running a commercial organisations is best represented. For example, the 5 August 1997 edition of the *Daily Telegraph* quoted Marjorie Scardino, chief executive of the media group Pearson, as saying: 'Pearson's goal is to achieve double-digit growth in earnings per share every year and to double the share price within five years.' This certainly suggests the belief that the share price is predominantly driven by EPS, but also looks at the process in a relatively long-term context. No comment is made as to whether the target also encapsulates the market-required return for the class of share.

Whatever the outcome of this debate, it should be clear that the chosen measures of corporate performance exert a fundamental influence throughout the system and ultimately on actual operations. The possibility that some could have an adversely distorting effect must be borne in mind.

Shareholders' interests seem to occupy a pre-eminent place in senior managements' 'who come first' thinking, even when other stakeholders are listed in mission statements. For example, in an interview in the *Sunday Telegraph* of 10 August 1997, John Mayo, shortly to become the new finance director of GEC, said, 'Putting shareholders first has transformed British industry and having that focus is vital.'

The presumption on the part of management that this should be so has been challenged by other writers such as Handy (1996) and Doyle(1994). They suggest emphasis should really be placed on securing objectives such as customer and employee satisfaction, rather than directly on shareholder returns, because successful achievement in these areas is seen as the true source of profitability. Acceptance of their arguments would lead at least to a rethinking of priorities within a performance management system, including executive reward schemes.

Without attaching priorities to them, the CMA Guidelines (ibid) lists several categories of core performance indicators (which should be capable of measurement) likely to be relevant to many companies. It comments that: 'because what drives long-term success varies from one business to another, it is not possible to provide a single template of performance indicators for all businesses'. The categories listed by the Guideline, together with examples of indicators for each category, are quoted below.

EXAMPLES OF PERFORMANCE INDICATORS
Society of Management Accountants of Canada, Management Accounting Guideline 31,
***Developing Comprehensive Performance Indicators*, 1994**

I Environmental Indicators
- Hours of community service
- Hours of industry activities
- Percentage use of recyclable materials
- Amount of pollutant discharge
- Accidents and injuries resulting from products or services
- Fines/violations of government regulations

II Market and Customer Indicators
- Share of market
- New and lost customers
- Customer satisfaction or dissatisfaction indices
- Quality performance
- Delivery performance
- Response time
- Market/channel/customer profitability
- Warranties, claims, returns

III Competitor Indicators
- Share of market(s)
- Customer satisfaction or dissatisfaction indices
- Quality performance
- Delivery performance
- Price performance
- New product development cycle time
- Proportion of new products
- Financial performance

IV Internal Business Processes Indicators
- Product development cycle time
- Number of new products
- Manufacturing cycle time
- Inventory turns
- Order-to-delivery response time
- Sales (production) per employee
- Non-quality measures
- Reinvestment indicators
- Safety performance

V Human Resource Indicators
- Employee morale
- Applicants/acceptance ratio
- Development hours per employee
- Employee competence measures
- Employee flexibility measures
- Employee suggestions
- Turnover ratios

VI Financial Indicators
- Revenue growth
- Market(s)/customer(s) profitability
- Product profitability
- Return on sales
- Working capital turnover
- Economic value added
- Return on capital
- Return on equity
- Cash flows

Many of the examples, of course, cut across all business levels. As part of a balanced scorecard, they would be selected so as to provide executives with an overall appreciation of business performance focused on those key factors seen as important to achieving the main business objectives.

Some particular issues related to the measurement of business-sector performance are considered next. The term 'sector' is used interchangeably with divisions and additionally to denote subsidiaries and other defined business units. Like the corporate unit, these may be composed of sub-units, but essentially are the first-line operational groupings below the corporate level.

MANAGING SECTOR PERFORMANCE

Perhaps one of the main advantages of the use of EPS as an overall performance measure is that is readily links with others such as return and investment (ROI), return on capital employed (ROCE) and absolute profit, which are commonly used at corporate as well as business-sector levels within organisations. Hence little adjustment to accounting routines is required and a 'system' is apparently more readily created.

Today, however, companies rigorously monitor their cash flows at both levels as well – the framework enabling the projection of future cash flows and finally NPV should be in place. Selection of a rate of discount appropriate to individual business sectors could be problematic; managers brought up on traditional measurement/reward/reporting systems might also find adjustment to a new scheme difficult. Otherwise, though, a performance management system has to address similar problems whether based on traditional accounting routines or cash flow.

The following extract reinforces some of the points already made concerning traditional accounting measures, and also discusses practical problems such as valuation and transfer pricing.

DIVISIONAL PERFORMANCE AND TRANSFER PRICING
David Dugdale, *Management Accounting Applications: Practical Elements*, CIMA 1994

You may have noted at least a couple of references to the divisionalisation of major companies. First, in Johnson and Kaplan (1987) it was noted that:

> The final developments in management accounting systems occurred in the early decades of the twentieth century to support the growth of multi-activity, diversified corporations.

The particular innovation they had in mind was the return on investment (ROI) measure:

> Use of the ROI measure was expanded in the 1920s as the multi-divisional form of organisation evolved.

Johnson and Kaplan saw the ROI measure as playing a key role in decisions concerning the allocation of capital resources to divisions and in evaluating the performance of divisions and their managers.... If divisional managers are evaluated using the ROI measure then, not surprisingly, they become very conscious of it and may employ it when evaluating investment projects. In this context it is often known as 'accounting rate of return'.

Despite its widespread use, ROI does have important theoretical drawbacks. Most importantly, a divisional manager in aiming to maximise ROI might not be acting in the best interests of the company. Suppose that the manager's division is generating ROI of 20 per cent. The manager will probably reject an investment project generating ROI of 15 per cent even though the company's cost of capital might only be 10 per cent – so, if accepted, the project would add to shareholder wealth. Conversely, if the division were returning only 5 per cent ROI, a project which would yield an ROI of 8 per cent would probably be accepted even though it failed to match the company cost of capital of 10 per cent. This is a classic case of a control system giving rise to a failure of goal congruence.

The shortcomings of ROI have led to the development of an alternate measure, 'residual income', which does not suffer from these drawbacks. Arguably, residual income (RI) is theoretically sound and, in the long run, maximisation of RI would lead to the same decisions as a policy of maximising discounted cash flow net present value [if an appropriate cost of capital were used (editor's comment)].

While RI is theoretically preferred it is much less used than ROI and, if *either* measure is employed, a number of issues have to be resolved, in particular:

- Should liabilities be deducted from the asset base?
- Should fixed assets be valued at historic cost, net book value or an 'appraised value'?
- Should opening, average or closing investment values be used?
- How should the income figure be derived and should it be before or after tax?

If a company is divisionalised it is usual for the divisions to sell product to each other. If this is the case, it becomes necessary to set transfer prices for inter-divisional sales and purchases. The theoretical issues which arise in setting transfer prices can be quite complex, particularly because such prices will affect:

- divisional profits and hence managerial motivation
- performance measurement
- goal congruence and autonomy

DIVISIONAL PERFORMANCE APPRAISAL

There are a number of reasons for divisionalising operations:

- management has specialised knowledge ;
- decisions can be taken more rapidly by more expert managers ;
- management is more highly motivated because they are responsible for both profits and investment – they feel more 'ownership' of the business.

In a sense divisionalisation can be seen as an evolution of the organisation whereby managers can be given responsibility for costs (cost centre managers), then profits (profit centre managers) and finally profit and investment (investment centre managers). A division can be regarded as a very large investment centre. If managers are responsible for both profit and investment then the measure of performance logically would include both these components – as do the two most common recommendations, return on investment (ROI) and residual income (RI).

It is presumed that you are familiar with the method of calculating ROI and RI. However, you may not be so familiar with the assumptions which underlie these calculations; these were addressed by David Woodward in May 1991. He took, as a starting point, the questions originally raised by Solomons:

- Is total assets, net assets (i.e. total assets less total liabilities), or fixed assets plus current assets the correct interpretation of divisional investment?
- Should fixed assets be included at historic cost, net book value or an 'appraised' value?
- How should centrally held assets, or those shared by divisions, be treated?
- Should inventories valued on a LIFO basis be adjusted?
- Should the investment base be calculated at the beginning or end of the period, or is an average figure more appropriate?
- How should the income figure be derived?
- Is a before- or after-tax calculation the most appropriate?

Woodward dismisses two of these items as relatively straightforward. LIFO, not being a prevalent method of inventory valuation in the UK, is dismissed. And Woodward argues that average investment should be used in preference to a value at the beginning or end of a period (on the basis that investment in a division will include retained earnings if these are not remitted to the centre, and it would not be unreasonable to assume that such earnings have increased regularly throughout the year).

Woodward addresses the remaining issues in more detail.

Which assets to include as the investment base

Total or net?

Solomons had contradictory views on this issue. He argued that total assets should be used as it was not necessary to know how the capital being used to finance a division had been raised. However, he also argued that, if stock was financed by increased credit from a supplier, the two factors should be allowed to offset each other. Woodward argues that, since the group will see the division as a shareholder would, the key question is whether the division is earning a satisfactory return on the group's investment. All controllable liabilities, both short term (e.g. creditors) and long term (e.g. debentures if the division raises external finance), should therefore be deducted from the asset base, and, arguably, a net asset approach is technically the most correct.

Short-termism

Woodward makes the point that a manager would be unlikely to carry through asset divestment if a book loss would result. In the short term, such a transaction would impact profit to a much greater extent than the asset base and measures such as ROI and RI would be badly affected. One possible way to address this problem would be to value idle assets at their market valuation (thus avoiding a book loss if they are sold).

Leased assets

While a number of authors argue that leased assets should be 'capitalised' for the purpose of calculating ROI or RI, Woodward's view is that this is wrong. He argues that leasing is likely to be more expensive in the long term than outright purchase and, therefore, no adjustment should be made. Presumably, Woodward takes the view that in the long run a division that purchases rather than leases assets will show a better ROI/RI than a division that leases its assets.

Cost, net book value or appraised value for fixed assets?

The depreciation problem

Woodward notes that a constant profit stream generated by an asset appears to give rise to an increasing return on book value as the book value of the asset is gradually eroded by depreciation. One 'solution' would be to include the asset in the divisional asset base at cost rather than book value. Another solution, proposed by Solomons, would be to adopt the annuity method of depreciation. Neither of these suggestions is attractive, and Woodward argues that both are irrelevant because of the consequences of inflation. Profits tend to rise rapidly with rising prices while the asset base will rise only slowly. This leads to a particular problem when an attempt is made to compare the performance of different divisions with different asset/age structures.

Arnold and Hope suggested that asset values should reflect the opportunity cost of retaining and using assets. For assets in regular use, market replacement cost might be used, while market resale value might be used for assets which were not in regular use.

Woodward notes that actually identifying such replacement costs might not be easy and goes on to suggest that for one of the most important elements in the asset base, industrial buildings, the insurance value for replacement would be sensible. Such a value would be based on the lowest cost alternative for replacement and therefore would not penalise a divisional manager unduly.

The treatment of shared or corporate assets

It is argued that the apportionment of headquarters assets to divisions should be avoided. If charges for headquarters services are seen as a rent for the use of resources, then it is argued that including the capital value of the underlying assets becomes unnecessary.

Intangible assets

While intangible assets such as goodwill are normally written off as quickly as possible, this can lead to an understatement of profit during the writing off period. This can disadvantage divisions which have such intangible assets, and Woodward suggests that writing off over the conventional maximum period of five years (and perhaps a longer period could be justified in such circumstances) would reduce the disadvantages of 'buying into' profits via acquisition.

What is return?

Controllable versus uncontrollable profit

Profit before deducting uncontrollable and non-recurrent items is seen as appropriate for appraising divisional managers.

In order to evaluate the economic performance of a division it is argued that the division must ultimately bear its 'fair' share of central and shared overheads, and these would therefore be deducted from controllable operating profit to arrive at divisional net profit.

Before tax or after tax?

Woodward argues that, in those situations where allocation of tax can be made to divisions on a reasonably scientific basis, it may be appropriate to measure divisional performance on a post-tax basis. This would encourage managers to take tax implications into account when considering fixed asset acquisitions.

Conclusion

Woodward notes that, while superior techniques for assessing divisional performance might be developed, any technique will only be as good as the input data provided. He summarises the recommendations of his article (which are intended to limit the possibility of short-termism among divisional managers) as follows:

The investment base
- A net asset approach should be used with all controllable liabilities being excluded. No capitalisation of the value of leased assets should occur.
  Assets should be revalued at:
  – market replacement cost for assets in regular use, using index numbers to enhance historic data or by obtaining quotations from suppliers;
  – market resale value for assets that would not be replaced.
- Provision should be allowed for alternative assets to be specified if these represent a cheaper (though proved adequate) alternative to those inherited by the present manager,

using for example the 'modern materials clause' approach to the valuation of buildings.
- No apportionment of headquarters assets to divisions should occur.
- Patents and trade marks should be included at market valuation where these are realistically obtainable.
- Applied research costs, development expenditure and purchased goodwill should all be capitalised and written off over a limited number of years.

The income figure
- Profit after controllable costs should be used to appraise managers' performance. Central and shared overheads should subsequently be taken into account when determining divisional continuance.
- The after-tax profit figure should be used to more accurately measure the effect of divisional managers' investment decisions.

TRANSFER PRICING

Ken Garrett (1992) notes that transfer pricing will affect the following:

- *Divisional profits and motivation.* It is generally accepted that managers are motivated to pursue profits, whereas they are not greatly motivated to keep within a cost budget. If transfer prices are set high enough then, as a division sells goods to other divisions, it will be able to make profits. It changes from being a cost centre to a profit centre, and this should stimulate management to aim for better performance and should provide increased job satisfaction.
- *Performance measurement.* If a division's performance is to be measured fairly, it must be allowed to sell goods to other divisions at a fair price. In this context, 'fair price' will usually mean the open-market price – if one exists. Using the market price means that each division must stand on its own feet, as though it were an independent company. For example, if the transfer price is set below market price, then the selling division might feel penalised and the buying division would be 'feather-bedded'.
- *Goal congruence and autonomy.* It is usually assumed that the aim of group management is to maximise group profit. However, once divisions are given some independence they may make decisions that are not in the best interests of the group as a whole.

Unfortunately, the objectives of encouraging motivation, maximum autonomy and 'good' decision-making can conflict. The problem can be highlighted by considering a group which has two divisions, A and B. Division A supplies division B which supplies the external market:

For the group as a whole, profit will be maximised if output is set at a level where:

Marginal cost = marginal revenue

And marginal cost will be incurred in both divisions A and B so, for maximum group profit:

$$MC_A + MC_B = MR$$

However, only division B is in contact with the external market and so this condition will only be fulfilled if division B has all the facts needed to set output 'correctly'. This will be so if division B knows how much marginal cost has been incurred in division A, and this leads to the recommendation that the transfer price from A to B should be set at marginal cost. Unfortunately, setting a transfer price at marginal cost means that division A will then sustain a loss equal to its fixed cost. The 'right' transfer price for group decision-making therefore has unfortunate consequences for the motivation of division A management. Various approaches to transfer pricing have been suggested in order to overcome these problems, and these are summarised by Ken Garrett in a follow-up article.

1. *Variable cost/standard variable cost.* As each transfer price embodies just the sum of variable costs so far, this method is good for decision-making. However, actual variable cost has the disadvantage that if the producer is inefficient, then the inefficiencies get passed up the line; the divisions receiving the goods get lumbered. Standard variable cost is better as any inefficiencies stay in the transferring division and the receiving division starts with a clean slate. The main disadvantage of this method is that transferring divisions make neither profit nor contribution, so their motivation is poor.
2. *Variable cost plus lump sum.* On a day-to-day basis, goods are transferred at variable or standard variable cost. After each period a charge is made to the receiving division to cover overheads and profit. The charge can be based on some sort of apportionment of the total contribution.

   This method hopes to get the best of both worlds: stocks are transferred at variable cost (good for decision-making) and profits can be made by each division (good for motivation).
3. *Full cost/full cost plus.* This gives a problem because there might be plenty of profit for each division (motivation) but decisions could be poor as fixed costs and profit are mistaken for variable costs.
4. *Dual pricing.* Here, one transfer price (usually representing cumulative variable costs) is charged to the buying division, while another (which will be high enough to allow profit) is credited to the selling division. The selling division is thus motivated and the buying division has information it can use to arrive at proper economic decisions. Obviously, when it comes to consolidating the divisions, adjustments will have to be made.
5. *Market prices.* If there is a market for the intermediate product, then transferring at the market price is usually sound. It is good for appraising divisions as each is treated as though it were independent and, provided the divisions are efficient, they should be able to make profits.

SUMMARY

Traditional, accounting-based financial measures of performance still tend to dominate at the corporate and business-sector levels of commercial organisations. Newer financial measures, based largely on the concept of net present value, have only relatively recently made an appearance in practice, despite the fact that net present value has long been accepted as the cornerstone of financial theory. These latest measures have been adopted by a number of (generally large) companies in Europe and the USA, but not apparently as yet on a widespread scale. It is also probably too early to judge yet whether they have significantly helped to enhance performance by their effect on managerial decision-making. Many institutions besides the companies themselves, such as pension funds, also influence whether they will be adopted or not.

Quantitative and qualitative non-financial measures, for example those related to market share and consumer satisfaction, are widely in use today, but there is debate over which measures to emphasise; should financial returns be regarded as some kind of residual which will be realised if positive success is achieved in other areas? It cannot really be left to pure chance: financial links have to be recognised and evaluated before-hand, at least.

A NOTE ON THE 'NEWER' PERFORMANCE MEASURES

While adding to the latter criticism of accounting-based measures, the following article by Simon Caulkin includes some warnings against an ill-considered embrace of what he terms the 'newer metrics'.

STAMPEDE TO REPLACE THE PRINCIPLE OF PROFIT
Simon Caulkin, *Observer*, 12 January 1997

Not content with the welter of ugly acronyms much beloved of businesses as measures of performance, American companies are inventing yet more. According to a recent survey by the US Institute of Cost and Management Accountants, nearly two-thirds of companies are losing faith in accounting-based performance measures and seeking new 'value criteria' to get a better handle on their businesses.

Driving the stampede to the new measures (or 'metrics' as they are fashionably known) is the obsession with shareholder value, itself booted merrily along by the tidal swell of management share options. What performance measurements best correlate with movements in a company's share price? How can a company boost the share price and shareholder value?

This is much more than a debate about measuring performance. How companies measure value determines how they are run. In its golden years, for example, Hanson measured the performance of all its businesses in terms of return on capital employed. It worked – but only for a time. When the world and the stock market changed, Hanson didn't, and self-destructed on its own performance metric.

Michael Black, the vice-president of management consultancy CSC Index, tells of a bank that bought a growing life insurance firm and imposed a strict return-on-capital regime. It was the wrong test to use: any growing insurance company will eat capital because costs come early, whereas returns take longer. But management remuneration was tied to return on capital, so it fired the sales force and the firm stopped growing. After four years return on capital (and managers' pay) had soared – but the insurance business was worth half its original price. Says Black: 'The bank had in effect paid the managers to destroy the company.'

For many managers and investors the easiest and most familiar measure – profit – has long lost legitimacy because it is easy to manipulate and backward-looking.

There are several contenders for the new favoured measure, and they all involve measuring business cash flows against the cost of generating them.

Most fashionable is probably Economic Value Added, the offering of New York consultancy Stern Stewart, which boasts 250 corporate customers, including Coca-Cola and AT&T in the USA and Lucas Varity and Burton in the UK.

Its greatest rival is 'cash-flow return on investment', or CFROI, promoted by the Boston Consulting Group and HOLT Value Associates.

Price Waterhouse claims a rush of European converts, from banks to utilities, to its ValueBuilder, a software-based process that aims to provide a breakdown of the cash flow variables. It identifies seven 'drivers', which can be changed to show, for example, how sales growth or working capital will affect shares. Price Waterhouse says it can be used to incorporate shareholder-value principles into decision-making at both divisional and plant as well as board level.

Since all the methods are based on the same figures, the argument is not over arithmetical 'correctness' but managerial appropriateness.

EVA, being a yearly measure, is widely used in the USA as the basis for management remuneration schemes; CFROI, which gives historical trends, is useful for the investment community, while ValueBuilder, claims Phillips, is compatible with both while giving an added strategic dimension.

Although some companies boast impressive success using the new metrics, observers counsel against putting too much faith in one version. Each has advantages and disadvantages and produces different winners and losers. Monsanto, the US chemicals company, uses both EVA and CFROI as well as a 'balanced scorecard' of non-financial measurements to assess its performance.

But how useful are the new metrics? At Warwick Business School, accounting lecturer Dr Brendan MacSweeney notes the 'narrow economic motivation' while Dr Peter Johnson of Balliol College, Oxford, points out that the causal link between strategic choices and share price is still unproven. CSC Index's Black warns that off-the-peg value systems end up consuming their champions if they are not adapted over time. The bravest companies, he says, invent their own metric and sell it to their stakeholders.

Guide to the new management argot
- *Added Value:* The difference between the market value of a company's output and the cost of its inputs.
- *Economic Value Added:* 'Economic' profit, or the difference between a company's post-tax operating profit and the cost of the capital invested in the business.
- *Market Value Added:* The difference between a company's market capitalisation and the total capital invested – thus the stock market wealth created (assuming positive MVA).
- *CFROI:* Compares inflation-adjusted cash flows to inflation-adjusted gross investments to find cash-flow return on investment.
- *Total Shareholder Return:* What the shareholder actually gets, i.e. changes in capital value plus dividends.

APPENDIX

The following was presented as a research discussion paper at the European Accounting Association Conference, Birmingham, May 1995. It provides a brief outline of the main concepts referred to in the preceding article as the 'new management argot' and how, in particular, the Stern Stewart performance measures of 'economic value added' (EVA) and 'market value added' (MVA) might be interpreted and applied. The results of applying these measures to actual data are also compared with those derived from the traditional accounting measure of 'earnings per share'. The paper represents an early stage of a continuing research programme dealing with performance measurement, but serves as an introduction to these ideas and some of the accountancy behind them.

ADOPTING PERFORMANCE MEASURES THAT COUNT: CHANGING TO A SHAREHOLDER VALUE FOCUS

J B Coates, M L Davies, E W Davis, A Zafar and T Zwirlein, European Accounting Association Conference, 1995

Shareholder value is now a well-accepted and often-discussed goal of most companies. Annual reports regularly expound on the virtue of creating value for shareholders and include it as an important corporate objective. The objective is achieved when the capital employed in the business earns a rate of return that exceeds the cost of obtaining funds. Although the shareholder value objective appears to be widely accepted by accountants, financial economists, strategists and others, it is often not implemented because management frequently becomes preoccupied with other objectives such as growth, market share, size, or accounting returns. Growth, market share, and size objectives may well be achieved at a great reduction in value to shareholders.

An increase in size and rapid growth is often highly correlated with higher managerial compensation, prestige, and executive perks but less highly correlated with an increase in shareholder value (Baumol 1961, Williamson 1963). Jensen and Meckling (1976) use agency theory to show how the self-serving managerial interest can result in the consumption of excessive perquisites and a reduction in the value of the company. Moreover, the diversification and acquisition strategies of the 1980s which resulted in hundreds of combinations are propelling the value increasing restructuring, spin-offs, and downsizing that has occurred in the 1990s (Bhide 1993).

At the same time, the many shortcomings of traditional accounting-based performance and return measures have been well documented (see, for example, Reece and Cool, 1978; Scapens and Sale, 1987; Ezzamel and Hart, 1989). Accounting numbers have been criticised for being backward-looking, open to manipulation and providing a poor measure of the outcome of company activity and implemented strategy (Kay, 1976). Moreover, as illustrated by Coates, Davis, Emmanuel, Longden and Stacey (1993), these measures are also likely to cascade down through a company's organisation to be applied to business unit performance. A further problem arises to the extent that external analyses of company performance are also based on accounting measures. The widely reported use of earnings per share is particularly prone to abuse through adoption of different accounting procedures (see Rappaport, 1986; Brealey and Myers, 1991; Stewart, 1991).

Other measures closely associated with EPS such as ROA, ROI, and ROE suffer from the same problems (Fisher and McGowan, 1983). Empirical analyses using accounting ROE as a surrogate for economic rate of return have been labelled as 'totally misleading enterprises' (Fisher and McGown, 1983:91) and of 'doubtful value' (Bentson, 1985:64). Jacobson (1987) analysed the relationship between annual stock return and accounting ROI and found an R^2 of only 2 per cent, showing that such accounting returns are poor measures to use in designing compensation schemes to reward managers for creating shareholder value.

In the last few years, a new measure, economic value added (EVA),[1] has been advocated as a better measure to assess corporate performance and shareholder value creation. As Stewart puts it, 'EVA is an estimate, however simple or precise, of a business's true economic profit' (Stewart 1994, p.73). The simplest definition of EVA is operating profits after taxes less a charge for capital used to generate these profits. The residual is EVA. If EVA is positive, the company has earned a greater return on the capital employed than the opportunity cost associated with the use of the capital. If EVA is negative the return on capital is not adequate to cover its cost.

EVA as a profit measure has a number of important advantages over traditional accounting measures. One advantage of the measure is that 'true economic performance' is determined only after making an explicit risk-adjusted charge for the capital employed in the business. Thus, advocates assert that EVA provides a superior measure of the year-to-year value that the business creates. Additionally, since EVA is a value measure of performance it should be used as the focus of the financial management system. Advocates contend that EVA should be the cornerstone of a financial system used to set corporate strategy, to evaluate new capital investment, acquisitions and company performance, and to determine annual bonuses for executives. Critics contend that although EVA may be theoretically sound, it is difficult and complex to put into practice since it often requires significant and somewhat arbitrary adjustments to the standard set of accounting numbers.[2] This study addresses the extent of the adjustments required to accurately measure EVA. We examine the trade-off between accuracy and measurement cost. Specifically, we examine several competing definitions of EVA from a very simple measure to a more precise definition requiring several adjustments. These alternative measures of EVA are then compared to determine whether the simple measure or a more complex measure is required to obtain a useful and consistent appraisal of performance.

We examine this question by establishing a benchmark definition for EVA based on some standard adjustments recommended by Stewart (1991). This outcome is then compared with two alternative EVA definitions that are less complex and simpler to calculate. Rank correlation coefficients and paired comparison t-tests are then calculated to determine whether the alternative definitions have a material impact on EVA.

Associated with EVA is market value added or MVA. MVA is defined as the company's market value (stock prices times shares outstanding) minus the economic book value of the capital employed. Stewart argues that MVA is a superior means of assessing a company's overall value-creating performance. Simply focusing on the total value of a company is inadequate, since, as Stewart states, 'a company's total value could be maximised simply by investing as much capital in it as possible'. Unless a company generates a sufficient return on capital invested, shareholder value will be destroyed.

In theory, MVA is the present value of expected future EVA. Therefore, Stewart argues, companies that maximise EVA should also maximise MVA, thereby maximising shareholder value. However, given that MVA is essentially a forward-looking measure, whereas EVA is historical, EVA performance may only partly explain changes in MVA. We examine the degree of associations between EVA and MVA for the twelve companies in our study.

We also calculate MVA using the two definitions of capital used in the three EVA methods and rank the companies in the study each year by these alternative definitions. We perform this analysis over time to determine how a company's rank is affected by the relative precision of the calculation for economic book value of capital. If rank is unaffected, the simpler and more cost-effective measure of economic capital may be preferred when calculating and ranking companies based on MVA. Given the earlier discussion of EPS and the preferential use of EVA, we have also considered the degree of association between growth in EPS and growth in EVA and MVA. In the following section, we describe the sample used in the study and the specific method.

Description of the sample and method

Given the preliminary nature of this study and the relative complexity of a precise calculation of EVA we have limited the sample to only 12 UK companies over a five-year period. The companies in the sample are all large UK quoted companies, and the majority are included in the FTSE-100 index. EVA calculations are performed for each year in the five-year period 1989/90 to 1993/94.

Three definitions of EVA are used in the analysis, each of which involves a calculation of net operating profits after tax less a charge for the capital used to generate those profits:

	£
Net operating profits after tax	x
Less: Cost of capital × Opening capital	x
Economic value added	x

The same cost of capital calculations are used in each of the three EVA methods, and therefore the differences between the three methods arise due to the respective definitions of net operating profits after tax (NOPAT) and capital used. Table 1 provides a summary of the calculations required in each method. (The method used to determine the relevant cost of capital figures is discussed below.)

EVA 1

EVA 1 represents the benchmark definition of EVA, which is a relatively precise calculation involving a number of adjustments to profits and capital as disclosed in a company's financial statements. The adjustments made are largely consistent with the method recommended by Stewart (1991).

NOPAT is calculated based on profits available to ordinary shareholders subject to a series of amendments. Firstly, returns to providers of non-equity finance are adjusted for. Hence, an adjustment is made to add back any minority interest and preference dividends, as well as net interest payable.

Further adjustments are then made with respect to non-recurring items, research and development expenditure, provisions and, where applicable, goodwill.

Capital is based on the total debt and equity financing employed by a company, including provisions. Equity includes the balance sheet amounts for capital and reserves and minority interest, as well as adjustments with respect to goodwill and research and development. Stewart argues that the resulting NOPAT gives a closer approximation to the underlying economic performance of the company than traditional accounting definitions of profit. Stewart also argues that the resulting capital figure gives a closer approximation to the underlying capital invested in a company, and on which adequate returns are required by investors.

EVA 2

EVA 2 is a simplified version of EVA 1, which requires few adjustments to reported figures and can be calculated relatively quickly. NOPAT is calculated as profits available to ordinary shareholders subject to an adjustment for net interest payable (per EVA 1). The resulting profit figure represents a broad estimate of net operating profits after tax.

Capital is calculated as debt plus capital and reserves, all as reported in the company's balance sheet.

Table 1: Description of methods for calculating EVA

	£
EVA 1 (Precise)	
Calculation of net operating profits after tax (NOPAT):	
Profit available to ordinary shareholders	X
Add: Returns to providers of non-equity finance	X
Adjust for non-recurring items	X
Adjust for research and development	X
Adjust for provisions	X
Adjust for goodwill	X
NOPAT	**X**
Calculation of capital:	
Debt	X
Provisions	X
Adjusted capital and reserves	X
CAPITAL	**X**
EVA 2 (Simplified)	
Calculation of NOPAT	
Profit available to ordinary shareholders	X
Less: Interest	(X)
NOPAT	X
Calculation of capital:	
Debt	X
Capital and reserves	X
CAPITAL	X
EVA 3 (Based on cash-flow statement)	
Operating cash flow	X
Less: Depreciation	(X)
Less: Interest	(X)
Less: Tax	(X)
NOPAT	(X)
Calculation of capital:	
As per calculation for EVA 2	

EVA 3

EVA 3 uses a definition of EVA which, again, can be applied relatively quickly and with few adjustments to reported numbers. It uses the same definition of capital as in EVA 2, but relies on cash-flow statement disclosures for the calculation of NOPAT. Given that one of the claimed objectives of EVA performance measures is to move closer to a measure of the cash-flow-generating performance of a company, we have calculated a definition of EVA which is based on operating cash flows less depreciation, tax and net interest. The justification for deducting the non-cash depreciation expense is that it is assumed to represent an estimate of the cash spent replacing capital stock which is necessary to maintain the operating capability of the firm.

Since cash-flow statements have only been required since the advent of FRS 1 (which applied to all accounting periods ending on or after 23 March 1992), five years' EVA 3 calculations are available for only five of the twelve companies in the sample.

MVA

MVA is calculated as the total market value of shares plus the market value of debt, less the economic book value of capital. In both MVA calculations, the book value of debt has been used as an approximation to the market value.

MVA 1 uses the same definition of capital as was used for EVA 1. This requires what might be regarded as a relatively precise and time-consuming calculation, involving a number of adjustments.

MVA 2 uses the same definition of capital used in both EVA 2 and EVA 3, which is relatively easy to obtain and requires no further adjustment to reported numbers.

Cost of capital calculations

For inclusion in the respective EVA calculations, a cost of capital, weighted for the relative proportions of equity and long-term debt finance, was calculated for each of the companies in the sample for each of the years surveyed.

The following considerations were relevant to the calculations:

Cost of equity

The cost of equity for each of the companies over the surveyed period was calculated on the basis of the capital asset pricing model (CAPM).

$$\text{Where cost of equity} = r_f + \text{Beta}\ (r_m - r_f)$$
$$r_f = \text{risk-free rate of return}$$
$$r_m = \text{return achieved on the market}$$

In this respect:

(i)   the risk-free rate of interest was calculated on the basis of the redemption yields available on twenty-year UK government gilts. In order to develop an ex-ante approach to the calculations, the five-yearly moving average yield up to and including each relevant year of examination was used in each of the individual cost of capital calculations.

(ii) following Dimson and Marsh, as quoted in Marsh (1990), a 9 per cent market premium was used, and

(iii) the beta values for each of the examined companies over the surveyed period were extracted from the London Business School Risk Measurement Service, the calculations therein being based on the correlation of market to security returns over a five-year moving period.

Cost of debt

The debt structures of the examined companies contained a wide range of both quoted and unquoted debt instruments variously ranging from long-term bank loans to convertible loan stocks.

In theory the precise cost of debt for a company can be calculated by identifying the cost of each element of debt – in the case of unquoted debt according to the fixed or market rate of interest (as appropriate) and in the case of quoted debt according to the return on the debt relative to market price – and weighting these costs relative to the relevant proportions of such debt held.

For the purposes of the current study, however, a market rate of interest, specifically the London Clearing Bank Base Rate, averaged for the five-year period up to and including each relevant year of examination, was used as a surrogate for the weighted average cost of debt. The market value of equity and the book value of debt were used to weight the respective equity and debt costs.

Statistical analysis

Rank correlation and paired t-statistic calculations form the basis of the statistical analysis of our data. The results are given in Table 2.

Results

The statistical test for the rank correlation coefficients is not very strong, the null hypothesis being that the true correlation value is 0. In all the rank correlation values quoted in the table, the latter hypothesis would be rejected at the 5 per cent level of significance in favour of the alternative, i.e. there is a correlation.

Table 2: Summary of results of statistical analysis

	Years*				
	1	2	3	4	5
Rank correlations					
EVA 1 v EVA 2	0.68	0.73	0.76	0.50	0.89
EVA 1 v EVA 3	0.73	0.63	0.42	0.41	–**
EVA 1 v MVA 1	0.08	0.01	0.24	0.13	0.40
MVA I v MVA 2	0.97	0.95	0.95	0.99	0.89
EPS growth v MVA I growth	–0 40	0.53	0.25	–0.07	–**
EPS growth v EVA growth	–0.19	0.31	0.43	0.25	–***
EVA growth v MVA I growth	–0 39	0.11	–0.33	0.13	–***
t-statistic values					
EVA I v EVA 2	1 27	0.51	1.29	1.31	1.37
EVA I v EVA 3	1.55	1.26	0.57	0.03	0.31
EVA I v MVA I	2.45	1.97	1.70	1.49	1.97

Notes:

* Where year 1 represents the most recent year used for the analysis (i.e. 1993/94)

** Only four years' data available

***Year 5 used as base year

The first two sets of values, EVA 1 *v* EVA 2 and EVA 1 *v* EVA 3, examine the relationships between EVA 1, the calculation of economic value added which most closely follows the detailed Stern, Stewart model, and the short-cut adjustments of EVA 2 and EVA 3. From year to year there is a certain degree of fluctuation in the values, ranging from 0.5 to 0.89 in the former case to 0.41 to 0.73 in the latter. While it is clearly true there is a notable degree of correlation in both cases, neither are consistently high enough to provide adequate justification for immediately accepting EVA 2 and EVA 3 as satisfactory substitutes for EVA 1 – given that the latter represents the 'best' assessment of economic value added.

The two following rankings, EVA 1 *v* MVA 1 and MVA 1 *v* MVA 2, represent a rather crude appraisal of the straight, year-by-year correlations of EVA and MVA values etc. These are regarded as preliminary workings only because the two sets of values, EVA and MVA, derive from different computations, the former being based on historical data, while the latter contains estimates of likely future outcomes. EVA may influence MVA, but it is not the sole source from which MVA derives; the nature of the relationship between the two requires further investigation, though Stern, Stewart do claim that a strong relationship exists. However, the correlation of MVA 1 and MVA 2 is very high indeed and would support an initial assumption that MVA 2 could be substituted for MVA 1 in order to reduce the number of adjustments to be made in deriving the value.

Of particular interest were the rankings of the growth of EPS and the growth in MVA and EVA, especially the former. Given that EPS is frequently seen to be a statistic in the overall performance of a company which ultimately drives the share value, a claim used to justify it as a leading company performance indicator, this initial assessment shows there to be only low-level correlations between EPS and either MVA or EVA. This would support the contentions of Stern, Stewart, as well as Rappaport and others, that EPS is a poor indicator of business performance. Again it has to be stressed that this is a first stage in the analysis of these variables. It also has to be noted that there is no better a correlation between growth in MVA and EVA, possibly for reasons already cited above.

Part 2 of Table 2 gives the t-statistic values for the differences in the values of EVA 1 and EVA 2, EVA 1 and EVA 3, and EVA 1 and MVA 1. The first two provide another view of the relationships between the different methods employed to calculate EVA, with the objective of determining whether the short-cut calculations of EVA 2 and EVA 3 could be satisfactorily employed as estimates of EVA 1, in place of the more comprehensive and more complex set of calculations otherwise required. Using a 5 per cent level of significance (a t-table value of 1.717 with 22 degrees of freedom, apart from year 5 for EVA 1 v EVA 3 where the limited data results in a t-statistic of 1.860 with 8 degrees of freedom), it can be seen that none of the t-values reach these levels. The test here is that there is no significant difference between the mean values (on the assumption that the variances are equal). This appears to be borne out, which could give some support to the suggestion that EVA 2 and EVA 3 could be substituted for EVA 1. Given the outcomes of the rank correlation calculations, further work will be carried out in this area, rather than reject the possibility that no substitution can be made which is sufficiently accurate.

The t-statistic outcomes for the comparison of EVA 1 and MVA 1 are more variable, but do show significant differences at the 5 per cent level in three of the five years. Again, this would lend support to the rank correlation evidence that these two variables are not well related on a direct year-by-year basis. Further analysis is required as to the nature and form of the relation between these values, given the claims made for them by Stern, Stewart.

CONCLUSIONS

In summary, the main objectives of this study have been to consider:

(a) the relationships between alternative methods for calculating economic value added and market value added,
(b) the relationships between economic value added and market value added, and
(c) the relationships between earnings per share and economic and market value added.

(a) has been carried out in order to investigate whether a simpler version of calculating either variable could adequately substitute for the more precise version of either. In all cases, there appears to be some evidence to support the use of the more easily computed versions.

The relationships in (b) are very weak, but the basis of these computations is acknowledged to be limited and requires further analysis.

Finally, (c), the lack of any strong connection between earnings per share and the two variables does appear to confirm the view that EPS is a poor reflector of the true economic values generated by a company.

Each of these areas of preliminary investigation is now the subject of further, more extensive analysis.

NOTES

1   EVA is a trademark name of Stern, Stewart and Co. for economic value added.
2   Indeed, Stern, Stewart and Co. has identified 164 different adjustments that potentially can be made to the accounting numbers in order to calculate EVA. They point out, however, that few if any firms would require all 164 adjustments.

REFERENCES

- Barfield, R (1994), 'How Much Should the Piper be Paid?', *Accountancy*, Vol. 113, No. 1209.
- Baumol, W J (1961), *Economic Theory and Operations Analysis*, Prentice-Hall, Englewood Cliffs, NJ.
- Bennett-Stewart, G (1991), *The Quest for Value*, Harper Business.
- Bennett-Stewart, G (1994), 'EVA, Fact and Fantasy', *Journal of Applied Corporate Finance*, 7 (2): 71–87.
- Bentson, G J (1985), 'The Validity of Profit-Structure Studies with Particular Reference to the FTC's Line of Business Data', *American Economic Review*, 37–67, March.
- Bhide, Amar (1993), 'Reversing Corporate Diversification', in Donald H. Chew, Jr, *The New Corporate Finance: Where Theory Meets Practice*, McGraw-Hill, New York.
- Brealey, R and Myers, S (1991), *Principles of Corporate Finance*, 4th edn, McGraw-Hill Inc., New York.
- Coates, J B, Davis, E W, Emmanuel, C, Longden, S G and Stacey, R (1993), *Corporate Performance Evaluation in Multinationals*, Chartered Institute of Management Accountants.
- Cornelius, I and Davies, M (1997), *Shareholder Value*, Financial Times Publishing.
- Doyle, P (1994) *Marketing Management and Strategy*, Prentice-Hall.
- Ezzamel, M (1992), *Business Unit and Divisional Performance Measurement*, Academic Press..
- Ezzamel, M and Hart, M (1989), *Advanced Management Accounting: An Organisational Emphasis*, Cassell.
- Fisher, F M and McGowan, J I (1983), 'On the Misuse of Accounting Rates of Return to Infer Monopoly Profits', *American Economic Review*, 73: March, 82–97.
- Garrett, K (1992), 'Transfer Pricing Explained', *Accountancy*, September.
- Handy, C (1996), *Sunday Times*, May.
- Jacobson, R (1987), 'The Validity of ROI as a Measure of Business Performance', *American Economic Review*, 77 (3): 470–8.
- Jensen, M and Meckling, W (1976), 'Theory of the Firm: Managerial Behaviour, Agency Costs and Ownership Structure', *Journal of Financial Economics*, October, 305–60.
- Johnson, H T and Kaplan, R (1987), *Relevance Lost: The Rise and Fall of Management Accounting*, Harvard Business School Press.
- Kaplan, R and Norton, D (1992), 'The Balanced Scorecard – Measures That Drive Performance', January–February, *Harvard Business Review*.
- Kay, H (1991), 'More Power to the Shareholders', *Management Today*.
- Kay, J A (1976), 'Accountants Too could be Happy in a Golden Age: The Accountant's Rate of Profit and the Internal Rate of Return', *Oxford Economic Papers*, 28: 447–60.
- Marsh, P (1990), *Short-Termism on Trial*, International Fund Managers Association.

- Porter, M E (1980), *Competitive Strategy*, The Free Press.
- Porter, M E (1985), *Competitive Advantage*, The Free Press.
- Rappaport, A (1986), *Creating Shareholder Value*, The Free Press.
- Reece, J S and Cool, W R (1978), 'Measuring Investment Centre Performance', *Harvard Business Review*, May–June.
- Scapens, R W and Sale, J T (1981), 'Performance Measurement and Formal Capital Expenditure Controls in Divisionalised Companies', *Journal of Business Finance and Accounting*, Autumn.
- Williamson, O E (1963), 'A Model of Rational Managerial Behaviour', in R M Cyert and J G March (eds), *A Behavioural Theory of the Firm*, Prentice-Hall, Englewood Cliffs, NJ.
- Woodward, D (1991), 'Back to Basics with Divisional Performance Assessment', *Management Accounting*, May.

Chapter 4

The Balanced Scorecard, Motivation and Rewards

INTRODUCTION

As performance measures/indicators are cascaded down through an organisation from the corporate level, through sectors to operational levels, their emphasis will probably change from quantitative, possibly predominantly profit-based financial, with some non-financial and qualitative measures, to being mainly non-financial and qualitative, with some cost-based measures. The problem of ensuring the system is positively integrated, that measures do not contradict each other, is obvious. Additionally, the number of measures/indicators which could be created is potentially very large: the wood might not be visible for the trees.

In the absence of off-the-shelf performance management schemes, managements must create their own, largely unique systems. Cullen et al. (1994) suggest that three key factors be kept in mind in designing a system: 'the dimensions of performance, the appropriateness of standards and the reward/penalty framework for managers'. Otley (1987) argues that 'regardless of strategic objective, operating environment and technology, any control system must address these three basic issues'.

The balanced scorecard, an idea introduced by Kaplan and Norton (*ibid.*), demonstrates how a logical, cohesive system might be devised which integrates financial and non-financial measures. The choice of measures/indicators to use within the scorecard, the avoidance of conflict between them and keeping their number to an essential, but adequate, minimum, remain problems for individual managements to solve. Some guidance to the latter is provided in the concept of the 'critical success factor'. Scorecards are generally developed for upper and intermediate organisation levels and should provide a fast and accurate means to appraise performance at each level. Departments and other units at lower organisation levels are more likely to have individual performance measures/indicators which should be seen to contribute to those used in the higher-level scorecards.

The Kaplan and Norton article is reproduced elsewhere in this series. The following is an extract from Fitzgerald and Moon (1996), which discusses further the factors quoted above from Broadbent as well as the balanced scorecard. The context is service industries, but the principles are general.

PERFORMANCE MEASUREMENT IN SERVICE INDUSTRIES
L Fitzgerald and P Moon, *Performance Measurement in Service Industries: Making it Work,* **CIMA1996**

The aim of this report is to give practical guidance on how four successful UK service organisations – TNT, the Peugeot Dealership Network, Arthur Andersen and Eversheds – make that crucial link between strategy and operations through the performance measurement system: *making it work.*

Simmonds (1981) coined the expression 'strategic management accounting' being: 'the provision and analysis of management accounting data about a business and its competitors for use in developing and monitoring business strategy'. The monitoring of company performance against those factors that are critical to its gaining and sustaining a competitive advantage should be an important component of any strategic management accounting system. Several frameworks have been proposed that explore the types of performance measures used at this strategic level. However, for an organisation to be successful these key performance indicators, defined in the language of corporate strategy, need to be translated into some system of performance measures used throughout the whole organisation, recognising that what gets measured gets managed.

In this context, the service sector poses particular problems for performance measurement. Frequently fairly junior personnel are in the front line delivering the service to the customer, and with the customer-oriented strategies adopted by many of today's organisations ensuring a consistently high level of service is difficult. The remainder of this section explores the nature and types of service businesses and introduces the *dimensions, standards* and *rewards* framework which is used in the review and evaluation section to compare the approaches to performance measurement in the four case companies. This comparison leads to some general observations regarding the methods adopted to make performance measurement systems work.

THE SERVICE SECTOR: SCOPE AND DIVERSITY

In a previous study (Fitzgerald et al., 1991) of performance measurement in service businesses three generic types of service organisation were identified: *professional services, service shops* and *mass services*. These archetypes span several standard industry classification sectors and were used to explore the way performance measures and mechanisms varied between the three service types. The case studies in this research provide examples of all three categories: TNT is an example of a *mass service*, the Peugeot Dealership Network represents a *service shop*, while Arthur Andersen and Eversheds are examples of *professional services*. The classification scheme is used here, together with the *dimensions, standards* and *rewards* framework, developed later, to analyse the performance measurement systems of the four case companies.

The classification scheme is presented below together with definitions of the service types. The three service types are differentiated in terms of the number of customers processed by a typical business unit per day against six other classification dimensions:

- people/equipment focus;
- front/back office focus;
- product/process focus;
- level of customisation of the service to any one customer;
- discretion available to front-office staff;
- contact time available with front-office staff.

In this classification scheme (see Figure 1) the number of customers processed by a typical unit per day determines the volume of demand placed on the service business. The other six classification dimensions detail aspects of the response to that demand.

Professional services are high-contact services where customers spend a considerable time in the service process. Such services provide high levels of customisation, the process being highly adaptable in meeting individual customer needs. A significant amount of staff time is spent in the front office, and contact staff are given considerable discretion in dealing with customers. The provision of professional service tends to be people-based rather than equipment-based. Emphasis is placed on the process (how the service is delivered) rather than the product (what is delivered).

Figure 1: Service classification scheme

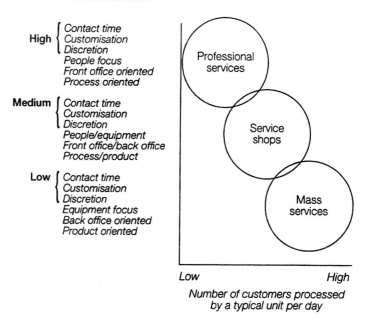

Mass services have many customer transactions, involving limited contact time and little customisation. Such services are predominately equipment-based and product-oriented, with most value added in the back office and restricted discretion available to front-office staff. The means–ends relationships are clear; the mainly non-professional staff have a closely defined division of labour and follow set procedures.

Service shops are characterised by levels of customer contact, customisation, volumes of customers and staff discretion, which position them between the extremes of professional and mass services. Service is provided by means of front- and back-office activities, people and equipment, and of product/process emphasis.

Obviously, not all companies will fit neatly into one exclusive category. Hybrids exist within companies: some business units may fit into the professional category – corporate banking services for example – whereas retail banking may be more closely aligned with a mass service company. In addition, as service strategies change in response to the current and predicted future environment, business units may move from one classification to another. Nevertheless, the kinds of performance measures and mechanisms used will be affected by the type of service unit.

Although service businesses have a wide range of service delivery processes, mixes of inputs and types of output, there is a set of four key characteristics which distinguish them from manufacturing businesses and influence the approaches to control and performance measurement (Fitzgerald et al., 1991). These characteristics are:

- simultaneity;
- perishability;
- heterogeneity;
- intangibility.

The production and consumption of many services are *simultaneous*; for example, receiving dental treatment or taking a rail trip. The customer has to be there during the process. Most services, therefore, cannot be counted, measured, inspected, tested or verified in advance of sale for subsequent delivery to the customer.

Second, if services cannot be stored, they are perishable. This *perishability* removes the buffer frequently used by manufacturing businesses to cope with fluctuations in demand. Controlling quality and matching supply to demand are, therefore, key management problems in services which are often exacerbated by the presence of the customer during the service delivery process.

Third, many services have a high labour content. Consequently, the standard of service may vary, the service outputs are *heterogeneous*. This places particular pressures on the measurement and control systems to try to ensure consistent quality from the same employee from day to day and to get comparability of performance between employees.

Finally, most service outputs, unlike manufacturing outputs, are *intangible*. For example, when buying consultancy services there are tangible measures of performance such as the completion of the project on schedule, but other less tangible factors such as the helpfulness and responsiveness of the staff which influence the overall level of customer satisfaction. Identifying what the customer values from the complex mix of tangible goods and intangible services makes the process difficult to control. Output measures such as the number of bed-days in a hospital do not necessarily capture the service provided or the benefits experienced by customers.

These four characteristics pose extra strains on service managers in terms of identifying what to measure and, in particular, when and how to measure performance.

THREE CENTRAL QUESTIONS

- What should be measured?
- How are standards set for the measures?
- What are the rewards for achieving the targets?

This section integrates existing ideas to develop a framework for reviewing how an organisation uses its performance measurement system to translate strategy into action. There is broad agreement that some form of performance measurement system is an important component of organisational control, and furthermore, that there is no general model that conveys a precise constitution of such a system. Different organisations will be pursuing different strategic objectives, operating in different environments with different technologies, and so will require different performance measures. However, Otley (1987) suggests that common to all systems is the need to answer three basic questions, which can be viewed as forming the basic building blocks of a performance measurement system.

1. What are the *dimensions* of performance that the organisation is seeking to encourage?
2. How are appropriate *standards* to be set?
3. What *rewards* and/or penalties are to be associated with the achievement of performance targets?

These three building blocks capture a total of twelve separate performance measurement factors which are shown in Figure 2 and which are discussed below.

Figure 2: The dimensions/standards/rewards building blocks for performance measurement systems

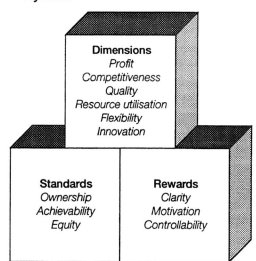

Dimensions

There is increased recognition that companies compete on a wide range of dimensions whose evaluation cannot be confined to narrow financial indicators. Simply focusing on financial performance can give misleading signals for the continuous improvement demanded by today's competitive environment. Important issues of customer satisfaction and establishing good employee relations would be missed by such a system. The challenge is to develop non-financial performance measures which capture the quality, service and flexibility issues of today's customer-oriented competitive strategies.

Common threads emerging from a review of three performance measurement frameworks – Fitzgerald et al.'s (1991) determinants and results matrix, Kaplan and Norton's (1992) balanced scorecard and Lynch and Cross's (1991) performance pyramid – are that performance measures should:

- be linked to corporate strategy;
- include external (customer service type) as well as internal measures;
- include non-financial as well as financial measures; and
- make explicit the trade-offs between the various measures of performance.

In addition, both the balanced scorecard and determinants and results frameworks distinguish between 'results' of action taken and the 'drivers' or 'determinants' of future performance (see Figures 3 and 4). The balanced scorecard complements 'financial measures with operational measures on customer satisfaction, internal processes, and the organisation's innovation and improvement activities that are the drivers of future financial performance'. The Fitzgerald et al. (1991) framework proposes that measures of financial performance and competitiveness are the 'results' of actions previously taken and reflect the success of the chosen strategy. The remaining four dimensions of quality, resource utilisation, flexibility and innovation are factors that determine competitive success, now and in the future. They represent the means or 'determinants' of competitive success. This is an attempt to address the 'short-termism' criticism frequently levelled at financially focused reports. It emphasises the notion that improvements in quality, for example, may not hit the bottom line in the current period but if these quality improvements are valued by customers future financial results should reflect this.

Figure 3: The balanced scorecard

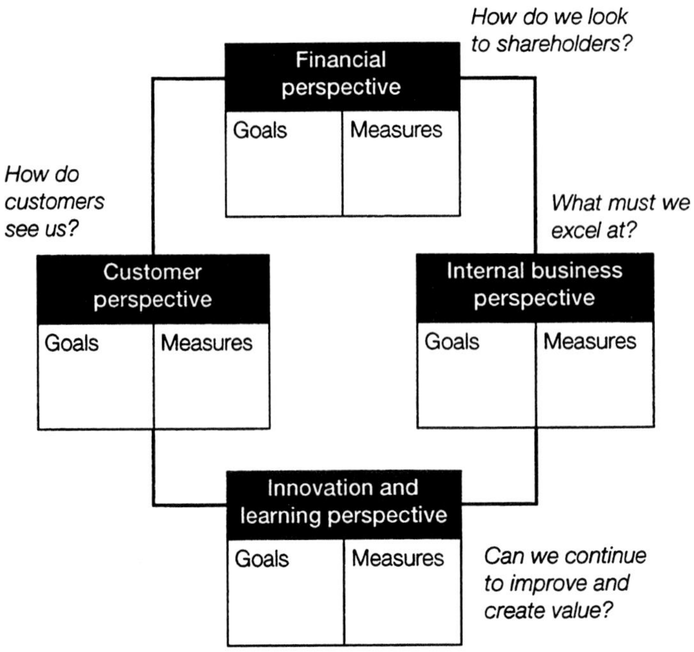

Figure 4: The results and determinants framework

	Dimensions of performance	Types of measure
RESULTS	Competitiveness	Relative market share and position Sales growth Measures of the customer base
	Financial	Profitability Liquidity Capital structure Market ratios
DETERMINANTS	Service quality	Reliability Responsiveness Aesthetics/appearance Cleanliness/tidiness Comfort Friendliness Communication Courtesy Competence Access Availability Security
	Flexibility	Volume flexibility Delivery speed flexibility Specification flexibility
	Resource utilisation	Productivity Efficiency
	Innovation	Performance of the innovation process Performance of individual innovations

An important feature of the three frameworks reviewed is that they are prescriptive in the sense that the dimensions of performance are specified, e.g. customer perspective and quality. However, actual measures of these dimensions will depend on the business type and, importantly, on the specific competitive strategy adopted by the organisation. That is, the types of measures used need to reflect, either directly or indirectly, the success factors that are critical to the achievement of corporate strategy.

Standards

The second building block relates to the setting of expected standards once the actual dimensions and measures have been selected. This involves consideration of who sets the standards (*ownership*), at what level the standards are set (*achievability*) and whether the standards facilitate comparison across the business units (*equity*).

Ownership

In establishing targets, the importance of individuals being responsible for owning the standards has long been established: this is often facilitated by the adoption of a budgetary system based on employee participation (see Argyris (*ibid.*), Becker and Green (1962)). This is considered to be beneficial to the organisation as it alleviates, or at least reduces, many of the dysfunctional consequences associated with traditional control models. In particular, managers who participate in the standard-setting process are more likely to accept the standards set (Emmanuel et al., 1990), feel less job-related tension and have better relationships with their superiors and colleagues (Hopwood, 1972). Participation does, however, provide opportunities for introducing budgetary slack.

Achievability

Research findings indicate that defined quantitative targets motivate higher levels of performance than if no targets are set (Tosi, 1975) and, providing the target is accepted, the more demanding the target the better the resulting performance (Hofstede, 1968, and Chow, 1983). Thus the budget level that motivates the best performance is unlikely to be achieved all of the time and adverse budget variances will occur. If adverse variances are treated punitively by management this may encourage budgetary slack (Cyert and March, 1963) where individual managers overstate expected costs and/or understate expected revenues, so that subsequent monitoring of actual outcomes presents them with a favourable evaluation (Ezzamel and Hart, 1987). Budgets need to be realistic enough to encourage employees to perform, but not set at levels so high they become totally demotivated. Finding the balance between what the company views as achievable and what the employee views as achievable is a frequent source of conflict.

Equity

Are the targets comparable across all similar business units, or do some have an inherent advantage unconnected with their own deliberate initiatives? For example, some business units may be subject to higher degrees of environmental uncertainty than others. Govindarajan found empirically that the higher the level of uncertainty, the greater the reliance placed on subjective judgement in appraising performance, with less reliance on objective, financial data (Govindarajan, 1984). It would be inappropriate and inequitable to treat the two extremes in the same way.

Rewards

The third building block relates to the reward structure of the overall performance measurement system. It is concerned with guiding individuals to work towards the standards derived above. It means posing three questions. First, does the system exhibit *clarity* to all those whom the system effects? Second, if you know what is expected of you, how are you *motivated* to achieve that performance? Third, what level of *controllability* do you have over areas for which you are held responsible?

Clarity

If one of the main purposes of the performance measurement system is to ensure the successful implementation of company strategy then this should be clearly understood by employees throughout the organisational structure. Research studies indicate that most managers react well to clear, unambiguous targets (Kenis, 1979) and acceptance of targets is facilitated by good upward communication (Hofstede, 1968). People should know what the organisation is trying to achieve, what is expected of them, and exactly how and why their own contribution, to the organisation's performance in meeting its objectives, will be appraised.

Motivation

In principle, employees may be motivated to work together for the pursuit of the company's strategic objectives by tying performance-related rewards, for example bonuses, to the attainment of key success factors. Goal clarity and participation have been shown to contribute to higher levels of motivation to meet targets, providing managers accept those targets (Hofstede, 1968). However, the effects of targets on motivation are complicated by the reward system and how it is used. Is the system used positively to encourage, or negatively to condemn, or both? When properly used, a responsibility accounting system does not emphasise blame. If managers feel they are criticised and rebuked when unfavourable variances occur, they are unlikely to respond in a positive way. Instead, they will tend to undermine the system and view it with scepticism (Hilton, 1994).

Controllability

The traditional view in responsibility accounting is that people should only be made responsible for financial elements which they can control (that is, have some influence over) and that they should only be rewarded for the results of their efforts. The implication is that managers would lose interest in cost control if their performance was being judged on events outside their control. From the viewpoint of the organisation as a whole, all costs are controllable and need to be controlled. The difficulty here is in pinpointing responsibility, particularly regarding the allocation of those costs arising from activities that benefit many departments or divisions within an organisation. Inevitably, the principle of cost controllability also involves the principle of the perceived fairness of cost allocations.

Evidence from field studies tends to refute the controllability principle described above. Both Merchant (1987) and Otley (1990) found that managers were held accountable, to varying degrees, for events and results over which they did not have complete control. The focus of evaluation was on how managers responded to events for the benefit of the business.

The service sector is diverse and is an important part of the UK economy. The characteristics of the sector present particular problems in control and measurement for service-sector managers. The dominance of customer-oriented strategies and the increasingly competitive environment faced by organisations demands that a range of performance dimensions are measured and linked to the corporate strategy of the company. This range of dimensions forms the first building block of a performance measurement system. Consideration also needs to be given to how targets are set for these measures and what systems of reward structures are used for achievement of targets.

In the next section the research findings from the individual cases are synthesised using the *dimensions/standards/rewards* model developed above as a unifying framework. This leads to some general observations regarding the methodologies adopted to make performance measurement systems work.

REVIEW, EVALUATION AND RECOMMENDATIONS

The main focus of this research has been the detailed documentation and discussion of the performance measurement systems used within four successful service organisations. In this final section we draw out the similarities and differences across the four case studies. We summarise each performance measurement system in terms of the *dimensions* of performance measured, the way in which *standards* are set as targets to be attained on those dimensions, and the *reward* mechanisms that are adopted to encourage high performance levels.

We summarise our research and suggest a series of general recommendations that represent best practice for the design of a performance measurement system. Following these general recommendations, we discuss how the specific characteristics of an organisation's system may vary according to service archetype (mass service, service shop or professional service). In the final section we offer conclusions.

Dimensions of performance
Figure 5 summarises the main dimensions measured by the four organisations across four categories of performance indicator. Profit and competitiveness are the results of corporate success (or failure) while quality of service and resource utilisation are determinants of success.

Figure 5: Dimensions of performance measured

	TNT	Peugeot	Eversheds	Arthur Andersen
Profit	By depot; publicised via league tables	By dealership	By office	By office and department
Competitiveness: *Market share at company level*	Informally	Published market research data	By relative size (i.e. no. of partners and fee earners)	Published UK fee income data
Market share at business unit level	Not measured	New car registrations by postcode	Informally through business providers (e.g. banks)	Informally through business providers
Quality of service: *On specific transactions*	Mystery customer, compliments files at head office	Mystery customer, post-transaction customer assessment	Case result, client evaluation interview	Client evaluation interview
Overall	7-star delivery performance league tables	Management inspections	Not measured	Not measured
Resource utilisation	Cost per consignment	Sales per employee, net profit per employee	Chargeable hours and chargeable fees per fee earner	Chargeable ratio, headcount

All four companies adopt a wide range of performance measures, both financial and non-financial. All too have some focus on the bottom line; profit remains critically important. The difference is in the way this profit information is disclosed. The mass service (TNT) regularly publicises branch profits achieved via the use of league tables, making overall success or failure immediately transparent to other managers within the business. In contrast, knowledge of profits is restricted to the partners in the two professional organisations, and to dealership owners in the service shop.

At the company level where data is available about the market segment as a whole this is generally monitored on a formal basis; thus, for example, Arthur Andersen is well aware of its position (and movement in position) in the UK in terms of fee income. At the business unit level, however, only Peugeot formally measures its competitive performance using a published breakdown of new car registrations by postcode. The others use informal mechanisms; for example, Eversheds will gain knowledge of how it is doing, in comparison with its local competitors, through the careful cultivation of relationships with business providers such as banks and insurance companies.

Considerable effort is devoted to measuring service quality in all four organisations. There are clear distinctions between the approaches adopted in the professional services compared with the mass service; these largely result from the intrinsic nature of the business undertaken. Both Eversheds and Arthur Andersen review their performance with (almost) every client. Some facets of performance are relatively straightforward to measure, the winning of a legal case or the successful completion of an assignment in accordance with the original job specification; however, these are output measures. The nature of the client/professional service organisation relationship is that projects often last a considerable time with a high level of interaction between the client and staff. The challenge is to identify problems early during the process, so that corrective action can be taken. This is achieved through some form of meeting, usually with the partner responsible, though the nature of the meeting will vary from client to client, with some wanting a formal interview-type setting while others prefer a discussion over a pint in the pub. The driving force is 'no surprises'. If there are problems, then the earlier they are identified the quicker they can be rectified, there is no point in waiting until the end of the process to discover that there were problems.

In contrast, TNT has a large customer base with each transaction taking a relatively short time. Service quality on individual transactions is assessed on a sample basis using mystery shopper schemes. These are output measures and the results are used to drive continuous improvement. In addition, overall reports detailing service performance over a wide range of measures are produced weekly by depot, in a league table format.

The system at Peugeot is a hybrid of the approaches described above. Overall service performance is measured by management inspection, with individual transactions sampled in a mystery shopper system and every new car sale followed up with a customer assessment questionnaire. This assessment is repeated twelve and twenty-four months after initial purchase, which, as discussed earlier, is entirely consistent with trying to develop a long-term relationship with the customer.

All four organisations measure resource utilisation at the business unit level, but a further determinant of success, flexibility, is not formally monitored, although all the organisations have strategies for providing it. For example, Arthur Andersen are able to pull in resources from other offices, if necessary, because there are consistent standards throughout the organisation, while TNT will employ subcontractors to meet early deliveries if capacity constraints are broken.

Similarly, innovation is not formally measured by any of the four organisations. However, there is a recognition of the need to continually innovate: for example, Eversheds' policy of sending out formal letters of engagement on every job has been introduced relatively recently. The innovation process does not lend itself to monthly reporting, but it is an issue regularly debated at business planning meetings.

Standards of performance

The framework earlier discussed three factors to consider in appraising the system used to set standards for the dimensions of performance.

- *Ownership* – do employees own their targets?
- *Achievability* – at what level are standards set?
- *Equity* – does the system cater for any variations between departments or branches that are outside the control of the employees?

Figure 6 summarises the standard-setting mechanisms used by the four companies across these three factors and distinguishes between standards set for profit and standards set for quality.

Figure 6: Setting standards for performance

	TNT	Peugeot	Eversheds	Arthur Andersen
Ownership: *Profit* *Quality of service*	Some involvement Centrally driven	Sales targets owned at dealership level Centrally driven	Set independently by office Centrally driven	Set independently by office Centrally driven
Achievability *Profit* *Quality of service*	Increasingly difficult Yes, via extensive internal benchmarking	Sales plan generally seen as achievable Yes, via extensive internal benchmarking	Generally seen as achievable Formal measures not set	Generally seen as achievable Formal measures not set
Equity *Profit* *Quality of service*	Allowance made for differences between depots regarding customer profile No allowance made for locational disadvantages	Allowance made for territory in the sales plan No allowances made	No allowance made for departmental differences in setting chargeable hours targets Formal measures not set	Not applicable Formal measures not set

There was a clear distinction between the levels of ownership of profit targets and service quality targets. Managers participate in setting the profit targets – to greater degrees in the professional service companies – generally through the business planning process. In some cases there was clearly an overriding view on what level of business activity would be acceptable. At TNT, a manager at one of the more successful depots described the ever-increasing targets as a 'fairy story'. In Peugeot, the negotiation is around sales targets rather than profit targets, a reflection of the franchise relationship between Peugeot and the dealership, with most of the dealerships being privately owned. Quality of service targets are almost invariably centrally driven, following the corporate viewpoint that a consistent level of quality should be apparent in any outlet of that business anywhere in the country. For TNT and Peugeot these measures are extensive and clearly defined. In the professional services the notion of service quality is more difficult to pinpoint. There is a clear view that a 'happy client' is important but breaking that measure down further is both difficult and probably of limited use, because different clients value different aspects of the service process.

Notwithstanding the TNT example referred to above, the profit and quality of service targets set are seen as being reasonably achievable. Within the two professional services, this partly reflects an acceptance of what is required of the job – 'as fee earners we need to attain a certain level of chargeable hours for the business to maintain its market position' – thus, the 'professionalism' of the fee earners leads to a positive attitude towards the targets. At the other two organisations, TNT and Peugeot, the perceptions regarding achievability are driven by the extensive use of internal benchmarking. This creates 'irrefutable' evidence (according to management) that the targets are realistic; if one depot or store can achieve a certain level of performance in one area then there is no reason why other depots and stores elsewhere cannot do likewise. Thus, internal benchmarks are seen as important in the quest for continuous improvement, and hence in sustaining competitive edge. Externally determined benchmarks, which in some ways might be considered preferable, are also monitored where appropriate: for example, market share performance. However, at a detailed operations level, comparative information is generally not available, and so external benchmarking is rarely possible.

Internal benchmarking also has implications for the equity of the system. It creates absolute, though continually improving, standards for service quality, with the ultimate holy grail of perfect quality performance – 100 per cent on-time deliveries, 100 per cent mystery shopper scores, or no late trunks to the hub. Formal allowance is not made for any systematic differences between specific sub-units. Thus, taking the latter example, the fine for a TNT lorry arriving late at the central sortation warehouse in Atherstone is the same whether it is travelling from Birmingham, 20 miles away, or Carlisle, 300 miles away. However, locational and other inbuilt differences are generally allowed for in setting profit targets. An exception is Eversheds where the target hours per fee earner remain the same regardless of the predicted effect of the economic climate on that fee earner's department. While litigation work may be fairly stable, property cases will fluctuate in accordance with the depth of the recession.

Reward mechanisms for achieving standards

In assessing the reward mechanisms used by organisations to encourage employees to achieve required levels of performance, there are three factors of importance.

- *Clarity* – do they understand what the company is trying to do?
- *Motivation* – what benefits, financial or otherwise, will they gain for achieving their targets?
- *Controllability* – are they assessed only on those factors they can control?

In Figure 7 the four organisations' performance measurement systems are summarised across these three factors.

One feature that stands out from our research is that in all case organisations, the employees interviewed exhibited a high awareness of the essential ingredients of their organisation's corporate strategy, and its implications regarding their own performance. Almost everybody interviewed at TNT emphasised the need to 'get the service level right', while at Arthur Andersen employees are left with little doubt as to the key characteristics necessary for a successful career path, given the comprehensive nature of the staff assessment procedures after every assignment undertaken.

In terms of motivation, it is perhaps not surprising that there is a noticeable pride in working for the company, as all are very successful organisations within their industrial segment. Arthur Andersen, for instance, is one of the top accounting and consultancy firms in the world, a fact that somehow adds to employees' self esteem. At Peugeot, there is also an evident pride in the product being sold, employees openly demonstrating a real love and enthusiasm for cars.

Figure 7: Reward mechanisms

	TNT	Peugeot	Eversheds	Arthur Andersen
Clarity	All employees very aware of the 'need to get the service level right	High awareness of Peugeot strategy at dealer level	Required standards of professionalism and service quality well understood though not explicitly stated	Required standards of professionalism and service quality stressed through extensive staff appraisal forms
Motivation *Financial (short-term)*	Extensive rewards mechanisms at all levels	Significant bonus on quality of dealership service	Partners' earnings dependent on office profits: no fee earner bonus scheme but pay rise linked to staff appraisal	Partners' earnings dependent on world profits: no fee earner bonus scheme but pay rise linked to staff appraisal
Non-financial	Pride in league table performance	Working in the business (a 'love of cars'); profit clinincs as support mechanisms	Prospect of making partner; respectable firm; good working environment	Prospect of making partner; working for the 'No. 1' worldwide accounting firm; high-quality training
Controllability	Non-matching of costs and revenues on consignments; full allocation of head office 'group service' costs to depots	No control over the product range – tied to Peugeot through franchise agreement	No controllability issues highlighted	Central costs allocated to departments

More concrete incentives are provided by monetary bonus schemes linked to performance. At TNT and Peugeot this is transparent with clear linkages between the performance level achieved and the amount of the bonus. At Eversheds and Arthur Andersen there is no bonus scheme, though it is acknowledged that a staff member's annual pay review is based in part on an assessment of their job performance. For these professional services the main incentive is undoubtedly the long-term prospect of making it to partner. Partners themselves, of course, have a direct financial stake in the business; their income depending on the profitability of the firm.

The controllability principle suggests that the performance of people should only be measured and rewarded on the basis of factors within their domain of control. Across the four organisations investigated the most striking departure from this concept was at TNT. Here, while several parties are actually involved in the service process for a particular package, only one depot receives the benefit of the revenue generated. Income is credited to the collecting depot, where the sale originated, rather than being allocated between the collecting and delivering depots, and possibly the hub as well. At times this results in some frustrations at the delivery depots, though there is an acknowledgement that for many (though not all) depots things balance out in the long run. The dual advantages of this method are its simplicity and its reinforcement of the teamwork ethic, important in a network organisation.

Performance measurement system recommendations
It is clear from the above comparisons that there are both similarities and differences in the way in which the organisations studied have designed their performance measurement systems. There is no single set of performance measures, no single basis for setting

standards for those measures, and no universal reward mechanism that constitute some perfect performance measurement system applicable in all contexts. However, emerging from this research are several themes which, together, represent common characteristics of the measurement systems adopted. We suggest that these serve as necessary preconditions for the attainment of best practice.

1. Know what you are trying to do

The starting point is to clearly articulate the overall corporate strategy of the organisation and then to identify those factors that are critical to its success. That is, the design of the performance measurement system must be rooted in an understanding of exactly what the organisation needs to do to exploit its sources of competitive advantage. This understanding should also be communicated throughout the organisation, so that all employees are aware of the company goals towards which they are working. In all four case organisations employees exhibited a clear understanding of their organisation's corporate objectives and image, particularly with regard to quality of service.

2. Adopt a range of measures

It is well understood that the traditional catch-all financial measures such as return on investment are inadequate for capturing the complexity of modern business operations. Organisations should adopt a range of measures covering six generic dimensions of performance: financial performance, competitiveness, quality, resource utilisation, flexibility and innovation. The performance measures used are likely to include financial and non-financial indicators, but should focus on the critical success factors identified above. In addition, the adoption of a range of measures helps to alleviate the potential problems of dysfunctional behaviour, notorious where managers' performance is captured through a single measure. Within each generic dimension of performance the number and range of indicators adopted will be highly variable depending on the nature of the organisation and its market position. At the Peugeot motor dealership network, for instance, the Lion Standards programme involves the evaluation of 71 separate factors within the operating standards component, just one of three components in the overall quality programme.

3. Extract comparative measures to assess performance outcomes

It is not always obvious what constitutes a successful outcome. Thus, performance measures need to be assessed against some standard. One possibility is to define the standards on the basis of internal benchmarking, so that the performance achievements of the 'best' units become the targets for all other outlets, leading to a culture of continuous improvement. As an alternative or as a supplement to this absolute performance comparison, relative comparisons can be made by directly displaying the results of all outlets in the form of published league tables. This use of league tables was noticeably widespread in the case of the mass service, TNT, where depots' relative performance is summarised weekly for profits and delivery, and monthly for finance and administration.

4. Report results regularly

For managers to be able to use the performance information proactively, it must be relevant and up to date. Organisations should be disciplined in reporting key performance measures on a regular basis. In the mass service and the service shop organisations investigated, key results are reported monthly and in some cases weekly, while Arthur Andersen produce reports after every job. This formal reporting mechanism leads to a large amount of information being produced but enables a faster reaction time in reproducing improvements and alleviating problems.

5. Drive the system down from the top

Finally, but equally importantly, it is imperative that managers throughout the organisation believe in the performance measurement system as representing a worthwhile use of their time and resources. This will largely be an exercise in corporate communication, but is likely to be most successful if there is a strong, well-respected corporate champion driving the system down from the top, who uses the resultant performance outcomes as a basis for regular dialogue between unit managers and the corporate management team. The successful design and implementation of the performance measurement systems at TNT is due, to a large extent, to the depth of investment made in them by the managing director.

For a performance measurement system to be an effective management tool, these five characteristics should, in our view, be key ingredients within any organisation. They represent, though, general characteristics, rather than a menu of specific performance indicators. The precise specification of a system will be contingent on many factors: for example, whether the organisation is predominantly manufacturing or service; the type of product(s) and production processes; the number of outlets; the degree of importance attached to the performance measurement system by senior management; and the ease of data measurement. Earlier, we discussed the three different service archetypes – mass service, service shop, and professional service. In addition to the contingent factors above, how then does this further factor of service archetype impact on performance measurement choice? Our research reveals that it appears to make no systematic difference. Turnover and profit are measured in standard ways, budgetary control systems are essentially very similar, and reward packages in the four organisations all display some combination of financial and non-financial mechanisms.

However, the one key area where service archetype appears to make a difference to the performance measurement system is in the measurement of service quality. The mass service (TNT) and the service shop (Peugeot) both monitor overall service quality through regularly published operations performance statistics. For the most part, this comprises detailed, hard, objective data such as the number of on-time deliveries or the number of late trunks to the hub. However, because of the high volume of transactions passing through the system, at the level of an individual transaction it is necessary to monitor quality on a sample basis. Thus, both TNT and Peugeot employ mystery shoppers to assess the quality and reliability of the service process. In contrast, the two professional services (Eversheds and Arthur Andersen) monitor service quality on virtually every transaction, usually through a client evaluation interview on completion of the assignment; that is, by adopting softer, more subjective performance indicators. The interview might be short or long, formal or informal, but whatever its format the firms will gain direct feedback as to the customer's perceptions of their service quality.

CONCLUSIONS

This extract has described in some detail the performance measurement systems adopted within four successful UK service organisations. A comparison of the organisations has been made using a framework of analysis, that addresses three sets of questions: what *dimensions* of performance are measured, how are appropriate *standards* set, and what *rewards* are associated with achieving the targets? These are the building blocks for performance measurement.

Our view is that there is no single set of performance measures, no single basis for setting standards for those measures and no universal reward mechanism that constitute some perfect performance measurement system applicable in all contexts. Generic dimensions of performance such as financial performance, competitiveness, quality and resource utilisation should all be measured. The translation of these generic dimensions into a set of performance measures will be a function of the competitive strategy being adopted and the type of service being delivered. Setting targets for performance will continue to be an area of lively debate. In our sample organisations, internal benchmarking is used extensively to defuse this argument, with the overriding message that there will be no compromise on quality targets. Rewards for achievement vary from tangible monthly financial bonuses to the more intangible 'feel good' factor because someone – a customer or a colleague – says 'well done'.

All of the companies were actively using their performance measurement systems to translate strategy into action. The systems and measures used were under constant review and had been changed, and will continue to change over time, as the focus of strategy changes. We recognise that the performance measurement systems reported here represent snapshots taken at a specific period of time in the organisations' histories and that in the search for continuous improvement some of those detailed measures may have changed. Nevertheless, what emerges from our research is a set of five common characteristics which we suggest are essential prerequisites for the attainment of best practice in the development of a performance measurement system:

- *Know what you are trying to do* – this must be driven by the corporate strategy.
- *Adopt a range of measures* – financial and non-financial.
- *Extract comparative measures* – there must be a benchmark for performance.
- *Report results regularly* – this discipline promotes knowledge and action.
- *Drive the system from the top* – senior management need to use the system.

In the context of 'executive information systems', Crockett (1992) describes a company's experience in establishing its own critical success factors and stakeholders' expectations, showing how these are linked to performance measures and benchmarking (the process by which the performance of key business areas/facilities is compared with the 'best practices' of other successful – world-class – organisations.

REVITALISING EXECUTIVE INFORMATION SYSTEMS (Part)
F Crocket, *Sloane Management Review*, Summer 1992

The process
To ensure that the right strategic information flows into its EIS, a company should:

- identify the critical success factors and stakeholder expectations
- document performance measures that monitor them
- determine the EIS reporting formats and frequency
- outline information flows and how the information can be used.

Before I describe the process in detail, I must add that it is complicated and time-consuming and that it involves all layers of management. Those who perform the operational activities that support the system must be involved in the development process. Researchers have noted how difficult this can be when management styles differ and people feel pressed to accelerate implementation.

Even so, companies increasingly recognise the benefits of taking the time to do it right. The following is an example of how a company successfully followed the four-step process. A manufacturing company established a task force of twenty employees from all functional areas to revise its performance measures and its executive information system. At the first meeting, the group brainstormed the information that would be pertinent to the company's critical success factors, which were quality improvement, increased flexibility, and quicker innovation. Then, for two months group members gathered the existing performance measures and screened them for usefulness. They found hundreds of measures that were being collected but that were strategically useless. For example, each month there was an internal headcount. But this was useless for reducing human resource costs because it did not include the large numbers of outside contract employees being used. The team winnowed out such measures and created a 'wish list' of measures that would reveal progress on strategic initiatives. For instance, quality improvement measures included the percentage of defect reduction, the percentage of scrap value reduction, and the number of product returns. Increased flexibility measures included the increase in multipurpose equipment and the percentage of employees cross-trained. Quicker innovation measures included the percentage increase in new product introductions, the headcount in new product design, and the investment in new product development.

The team presented its suggested measures to senior managers, who remained sceptical that the measures would really revitalise their decision-making. The team members determined that management was sceptical because they had not stressed the power of linking the multiple performance measures. They had not linked process measures with results measures or created cross-functional linkages.

For almost two months, the task force struggled with these linkages. They eventually came up with ways to use measure results to evaluate progress toward the strategic goals. For instance, they showed how an improvement in paint process quality and a decrease in the frequency with which warranties are exercised (quality process measures) helped to increase customer satisfaction by 15 percent (result measure). Senior managers began to be more interested in the project.

For its third presentation to senior managers, the team connected the data across functions, developing spider charts, bar charts, tables, and line graphs for each of the new measures. They sequenced the charts around the three strategic issues. Senior executives were stunned. They had never seen an integrated presentation detailing how well the company was progressing in achieving its most important goals. Only then did they acknowledge that the information would provide them with the ideas they needed to solve difficult business problems.

Without this process, the company would have continued to pump out mostly unusable information. The task force successfully developed an executive information system that graphically displayed precise information linked to strategic issues.

- **Step one: Identify critical success factors and stakeholder expectations.** The first step helps the team determine what information to collect. The team reviews budgets, business plans, and planning documents to identify current critical success factors. Senior, line, and function managers discuss the company's strategic goals and brainstorm new critical success factors. Stakeholder expectations, which are almost never explicitly mentioned in existing documentation, are brought into the discussion. At one company, we determined stakeholder expectations by interviewing the corporate staff members who regularly met with important stakeholders – staff in government relations, the legal department, investor relations, and so on. These staff members provided not only important information but also ideas about potential problems.

  A Fortune 100 company began the process by analysing how design and manufacturing affected its goal of low-cost, high-quality manufacturing. The team determined that the critical factor in the design process was simplification. Since the design process crossed multiple organisational boundaries – from research and development to design engineering to the plant that produced the prototype – the company put together a cross-functional team to analyse these connections. The critical success factor for manufacturing was synchronous manufacturing. Plant managers and manufacturing engineers analysed this factor.

The company also identified two critical groups of stakeholders. Consumers were most concerned with the number of repairs necessary throughout the product's life. At the same time, however, institutional investors were becoming increasingly vocal about receiving a certain return on investment. Improved cash flow was seen as this group's most important expectation. With this information, the company was ready for the next step.

- **Step two: Document performance measures that monitor the critical success factors and stakeholder expectations.** A company must identify the specific information that will tell managers whether progress is being made on the critical success factors and whether stakeholder expectations are being met. Currently, the idea of what makes a good performance measure – how performance measures should fit changing concepts of strategy and stakeholders – is undergoing a transformation in many companies. I believe that EIS difficulties stem from the same problems that have generated this 'performance measurement revolution'. Identifying the right performance measures is key to EIS success.

    Step two proceeds much like step one. First, the project team documents current performance measures throughout the company. Second, the team compares these measures with the critical success factors and stakeholder expectations and brainstorms new measures necessary to achieve them. Whereas the critical success factors are broad, the performance measures range from the general to the specific.

    For example, in the Fortune 100 company described above, the team brainstormed fifteen performance measures for determining progress on synchronous manufacturing. The measures ranged from the most general, including the number of inventory turns and the percentage of capacity utilised, to the more specific, such as the percentage of workers cross-trained within the manufacturing department. The more specific measures are the most difficult to design but can yield the most important strategic benefits. The performance measures often reflect the company's differentiation strategy.

    Measures should not only identify problems but help solve them. This company selected measures that monitored intermediate procedures that heavily influenced product cost, quality, and responsiveness. For example, traditionally the company measured quality by inspecting finished goods and calculating the percentage of end products without defects. The team established new measures to monitor quality at two key production processes. In particular, the team measured the ability of the molding and painting machinery to produce interim products without defects. Such 'down the line' monitoring pinpointed the sources of problems. Of course, although intermediate measures can help locate problems, a solution can be determined only when problems are traced back to their roots in the production process.

    It is important that performance measures linked to stakeholder expectations be as specific and realistic as those tied to the company's success factors. One company found two measures for the expectation of improved shareholder value: stock price plus dividends and return on equity minus the cost of equity over time. Figure 2 lists some other measures tied to stakeholder expectations.

Figure 2: Sample stakeholder expectations and related measures

Employees		*Shareholders*	
Expectation	**Measure**	**Expectation**	**Measure**
Good working conditions	Moral index	Improved shareholder value	• Stock price and dividends • Return on equity minus cost of equity

Government		*Customers*	
Expectation	**Measure**	**Expectation**	**Measure**
Conformance to environmental regulations	Percentage of products in conformance	• Product quality throughout product life • Dealer support	• Warranty cost • Number of profitable dealers

After measures have been brainstormed, the most appropriate ones must be selected. Participants in this process should ask six questions.

- Can each measure be externally benchmarked?
- Can each measure be tied to strategy and business plans in order to guide employee actions?
- Will the user understand each measure and be able to diagnose problems?
- Can each measure be easily calculated, thus reducing collection and reporting costs?
- Do the measures cover both processes and results?
- How do the measures work together as a group?

Too often, a measure is chosen because it is 'interesting.' A soft-goods manufacturer initially deemed a measure – the number of suppliers – appropriate because it could be externally benchmarked and easily understood and calculated. However, the project team rejected the measure because supplier rationalisation or multiple sourcing was not a company strategy. The measure was not tied to any strategic purpose.

Everyone affected by the new system – employees and managers – must be involved in these discussions in order to ensure buy-in. This is often the most difficult part of the process. At the company with the goal of synchronous manufacturing, the project team had brainstormed thirty performance measures. It took several months to winnow this list down to fifteen because of the disputes that surfaced among employees and line and senior managers.

Once measures are determined, they need to be refined. How exactly will they be calculated? Where will the data come from? Again, all affected people should be involved in these discussions, and conflicts are likely to surface. No one wants to look bad under the new system. In the Fortune 100 company, one dispute regarded the measure 'safety'. Plant managers wanted to calculate lost-time accidents whereas the central staff members wanted to calculate the cost of safety-related insurance claims. Only after several meetings was the issue resolved, with two specific calculations agreed upon.

Differences of opinion about the best way to calculate a measure often stem from differing ideas about what the critical success factors are and which are most important. I've seen these conflicts solved in several ways: (1) allowing the person or group with the most influence on the measure's result to make the decision; (2) using two different calculations in the system and running them both until it's apparent which is most useful; and (3) giving one person or group the authority to make final decisions.

After all of these discussions, the entire organisation understands precisely how it must change. Although some individuals may feel that they are not getting the information they need, most employees and managers should feel that their concerns were heard and responded to.

Now management has the task of setting goals for the measures, often using external benchmarks. Managers may establish stretch targets for employees. They may influence perceptions of importance by setting lenient goals for some measures and strict goals for others. Then they can review progress and identify performance gaps.

Further discussion of critical success factors comes from the CMA Guideline.

DEFINING THE CRITICAL SUCCESS FACTORS
Society of Management Accountants of Canada, Management Accounting Guideline 31,
***Developing Comprehensive Performance Indicators*, 1994**

Once a business model has been developed and the firm's goals and strategies articulated and made consistent with that business model, it becomes possible to begin to establish the comprehensive performance indicator system that will be used to monitor and influence progress towards the attainment of the firm's goals, strategies, and objectives. 'Critical success factors', 'key success factors', or 'key result areas' are labels that are attached to the idea that a limited number of critical factors drive the success of a firm. Focusing on the most critical factors will have the most impact and will drive accomplishment in other supporting areas.

For example, many businesses led by the Japanese but emulated by a number of North American and other companies have emphasised the importance of quality and reliability in their product offerings. Focusing on quality in the eyes of the customer and assuring that there is a process in place to achieve the highest quality leads one to the conclusion that tracking or monitoring quality performance is critical. At the uppermost levels of the firm, broad overall measures of quality may be monitored by tracking customer satisfaction or complaints. At lower levels, measures of quality of supplier inputs through the conversion process and at the end of the production process obviously reinforce an emphasis on quality. At the specific operation level, the statistical process control and other detailed measurement techniques reinforce such an emphasis.

Similarly, with such critical dimensions as speed, more companies are measuring response time to customers' orders in terms of hours, manufacturing process times in terms of days, and new product development cycles in terms of months. In all cases, they may historically have been considerably longer. With measures pertaining to costs, firms are applying new methodologies such as activity-based costing to eliminate wasteful activities. They are utilising activity-based cost management, business process redesign, and re-engineering. Generically, one can identify performance indicators that relate to the environment, markets, and customers; to competitors; and to the various internal business processes (such as market and product development, the supply chain, administration, investment, and financing processes).

Performance indicator systems will still include financial indicators. Such items as sales growth, profit margins, income and earnings per share, asset management, return on assets employed, capital and equity, and cash flow clearly will continue to be tracked. The purpose of any performance indicator system is to track those key driver categories that most influence management decisions and, ultimately, the long-term success of the business as measured by increases in shareholder value.

Firms must also think in terms of a hierarchy of measures. A limited set of summary measures directly responds to the most critical aspects of the business from the standpoint of top management. As one moves down in the organisation, middle managers responsible for horizontal business processes need to have indicators that are most significant to their process responsibilities as well as to key operations. Throughout the firm, additional indicators must focus on specific improvement.

A vital issue in the selection of the limited number of indicators for the firm is that in all likelihood only a few are truly critical. These should get highest attention and focus. There may be some other indicators that also should be tracked, as secondary, in the possibility that they may become, in fact, more critical over time.

Performance indicators need to be sharply focused on those aspects of the business that are most critical to achieving the long-term goals of the firm. It is a real challenge for many firms to de-emphasise, or actually give up, many of the measures being tracked, even though not important in the larger scheme of things, redundant with other measures, or actually counterproductive.

Examples of performance measures developed at the primary operational level of certain manufacturing companies are described in an article by Innes and Mitchell, which also serves to emphasise the dynamic nature of the whole process – measures must reflect changes in a business. Only a small extract from the article appears below.

PERFORMANCE MEASUREMENT
J Innes and F Mitchell, 'The Process of Change in Management Accounting',
***Management Accounting Research*, Vol. 1, 1990**

Cost of quality. Firms A, C, D, E and F had developed systems, of varying degrees of sophistication, to measure the cost of quality. While some of the firms were at a relatively early stage in the process their aim was to produce cost information on:

(i)   cost of prevention (such as design reviews, quality audits and supplier evaluation);
(ii) cost of appraisal (such as inspection);
(iii) cost of failure (such as repair and replacement of parts and products which fail after being delivered to the customer).

The costs gathered under (i) and (ii) above were normally grouped together as the internal cost of quality, and category (iii) was termed the external cost of quality. The actual costs were compared with a budget on a monthly basis and monitored to ascertain whether reductions in the cost of failure outweighed the costs incurred in prevention and appraisal.

Material cost and stock-monitoring. Specific reports on factors relating to direct material cost had been instituted in firms D, E and F. These took two forms. Firstly, the operation and stock predictions of the firm's materials requirement plan (MRP) were monitored and reported upon at monthly intervals. Secondly, detailed comparisons of expected and actual stock levels for all types of materials were produced. In firm E this latter type of report also included a surplus stock section which was circulated on a worldwide basis within the firm.

Non-financial measures. Non-financial performance indicators had become widely used within the seven firms. These had been developed by management accountants to supplement conventional financial measures by reporting specifically on such areas as delivery performance, absenteeism, launch time for new products, quality and machine performance. Firm D had developed a pyramid system of over 900 control measures which covered most aspects of the firm's activities. The performance measures at the top of this pyramid were mainly financial but the subsidiary measures used to investigate variations in the key measures included many non-financial measures which related to production, marketing and service function performance down to the level of key individual employees.

Firms E and F reported monthly on what its managers considered to be critical success factors. In Firm E new product launches and their success rate were closely monitored. In Firm F a major part of the supplementary performance measurement concerned customer satisfaction and was composed entirely of non-financial measures:

- on-time deliveries
- $\dfrac{\text{number of completed orders shipped}}{\text{total orders shipped}}$
- current sales order index
- ageing of past due orders
- percentage of products rejected in any way by customer
- product quality index.

Another area of non-financial performance where accountants were involved was that of machine performance. With the relative insignificance of direct labour costs and the capital-intensive nature of the high-tech sector, the performance of equipment was often more critical than the performance of the direct labour force. Management accountants in most of the firms reported on machine efficiency, breakdowns and downtime.

Landed cost and worldwide standards. A performance measure relevant to supply decisions was used by three of the multinational firms (D, E and F). It was termed landed product cost. Landed cost is the total cost of the product as delivered to the customer. For example, if the customer is in Turkey the total landed cost would include not only the unit cost of manufacturing the product in a Scottish factory but also the distribution, freight and duty costs of delivering the product to the Turkish customer. Firm E used a series of individual product landed cost curves (unit landed cost over the product life) to illustrate the changing cost of delivering its products to different countries.

Firms E and F also produced worldwide standard costs for each product manufactured. For example, the worldwide standard for a particular material was set at the lowest price at which that material could be bought worldwide. The standard constructed in this way was used to assess the relative cost effectiveness of particular plants. However, for operational control at the local level, adjustments were made to these standards to reflect local conditions.

Additional comment and an example on motivation and reward is provided by the following extract from Fitzgerald et al. (1991).

HOW TO MOTIVATE AND REWARD EMPLOYEES
L Fitzgerald, R Johnston, S Brignall, R Silvestro and C Voss, *Performance Measurement in Service Businesses,* **CIMA 1991**

It is a key management task to get all employees to work together in the pursuit of strategic objectives. Participation and shared responsibility are central to this. An organisation's management information system and any incentive scheme linked to it are important in this context in several ways.

First, many things may be important to competitive success and should be measured, but they need not be part of any reward system. As a result, reward schemes may focus on a sub-set of the performance measures in the management information system.

Second, while much of the information system may be intended to motivate and reward managers for those things for which they are responsible and which they can control, it may also be perceived as threatening. Because the information system may be used to threaten or reward, managers may be tempted to manipulate it. There is therefore a risk that any information system which is also being used to evaluate and reward managers may cause them to take actions which are strategically undesirable. This may also cause misleading information to be fed into the information system, so causing top managers to make mistakes.

There is no easy way to avoid these problems. Participation in the design and running of such systems is no simple solution, for while it may lead to their acceptance and to behaviour congruent with organisational goals, it may also lead to playing the system and the building-in of unsuitable performance measures and targets. Individuals will differ in this respect, perhaps unpredictably.

The safest way of proceeding therefore is to tie performance-related rewards, for example bonuses, to the attainment of key success factors by groups of managers within an SBU and across the whole organisation (to give a rationale for co-operative interrelationships). In other words, rewards accrue to individuals but should be earned by group success. Finally, the key success factors that will determine the bonuses should be linked to *determinants* of competitive success, such as service quality, as well as to *results* such as profitability. BAA is cited as an example of the successful use of a senior management bonus system.

BAA plc

Since privatisation as a near-monopoly the pressure on BAA to demonstrate publicly that financial performance is being maintained without detriment to service quality has, if anything, increased. BAA's control and performance measurement systems are therefore designed to give both financial and non-financial information at all organisational levels, with particular stress on four strategically key areas: *provision and utilisation of capacity, generation of income, utilisation of manpower* and *standards of service* provided to airport users. The management bonus scheme is linked to both financial performance and service levels. (Financial performance will, at least to some degree, subsume the first three key factors. Thus, while manpower utilisation, for example, is strategically important and is therefore measured, it is not a formal part of the bonus system.) For each airport, the bonus is calculated on the basis of performance against a profit target, but even if this target is met it is possible for no bonus to be paid. The reason for this is that targets are also set for five key measures of customer satisfaction, and 20 per cent of the bonus is cut for every such target unmet.

This is an interesting and effective combination of a measure of results and five measures of determinants of competitive success being used in the design and operation of a bonus system.

SUMMARY

The aim of this chapter has been to show how a balanced performance management system may be created. It emphasises the need for the system to be cohesive, with logical links to the various levels throughout an organisation. Critical success factors serve to focus the system; benchmarking assists in setting targets for achievement. Although examples are given of performance measures/indicators, many of which in essence will be common to a wide range of organisations, the determination of the actual structure of a system and the specific measures employed is the responsibility of individual managements.

For some useful further reading Moizer's chapter in Ashton et al. (1991) contains interesting comment on performance and reward mechanisms. He also points out the role which management accountants may have in the creation and operation of these systems.

A NOTE ON QUANTITATIVE AND QUALITATIVE EVALUATION

Objectives and measures may be formulated and monitored throughout an organisation using a mixture of quantitative and increasingly qualitative information. The article by Harvey (1984) quoted below provides a general background and guidance on the handling of information and the ways in which qualitative information can sometimes be quantified.

BALANCING FACTS AGAINST FIGURES (part)
Michael Harvey, *Certified Accountant*, July 1984

Information gatherers must learn to consider the concept of opportunity costs and the use of cost-benefit techniques. The latter approach involves the use of qualitative, as well as quantitative, information. By using these concepts and techniques, information which is *relevant* will be collected and analysed. If historic information does turn out to be the same as the information which is relevant to the decision at hand, this will merely be coincidental.

The need for relevant information applies whether the decision concerns the short term, as in the case of many pricing decisions, or the medium to long term, such as when an investment decision is to be made. Whatever the decision being considered, the aim must be to identify the information associated with the alternative courses of action which could be taken. This will enable the decision-maker to arrive at what is felt to be the 'best' decision.

For many reasons, various categories of information can be considered to be irrelevant to a particular decision analysis. This means that when costs are being clarified for decision purposes, care needs to be taken to highlight the pertinent information involved. Neither historic information nor *all* the information available will necessarily be relevant to a particular decision. Information which is irrelevant should be eliminated from the analysis.

An example of information which is non-relevant is provided when a choice has to be made between alternative courses of action. In such a situation costs which are common to all the feasible pathways associated are not relevant to the decision. For example, if the same space in the workshop could be used to produce one of a number of different products then, as the value of this space is common to the manufacture of all the products that could be made, its cost is not relevant to a decision concerning which product should be produced. Such common costs should therefore be omitted from the decision analysis.

Another example of information that is not relevant concerns sunk costs. As these cause no future out-of-pocket expenditure, in so far as they have no remaining value associated with them, they are irrelevant except to the extent of any associated opportunity costs. Thus a retailer who has paid a quarter's rent in advance, with three months to go on a lease before a redeveloper takes repossession of the leased building, and with no chance of selling the tail end of this lease, needs to understand that the amount already paid as rent for this final quarter has no relevance to the decision regarding the continuation of trading during the final three months.

An approach of separating out information relevant to a decision is helpful because it clarifies and highlights the data presented to the decision-taker. It forces that person to focus on the key issues of the problem. A relevant cost *must* involve some future payment or loss in value if the decision-maker were to take a particular course of action.

Although past costs are frequently extrapolated to enable the accountant to forecast future cost levels, it is nevertheless important to realise that (apart from the possible benefits that past costs may give when they are incorporated into some forecasting models), historic cost information is usually completely irrelevant to the decision-maker. Sometimes when supplying relevant information to decision-makers the concept of dual prices can be used to show that even the current cost price of an asset owned by an enterprise does not necessarily provide information on the relevant 'value' of that resource to the organisation.

A simple definition of a *relevant cost* is 'a cost which is expected to occur and which is different from the other costs in other possible alternative courses of action being considered'.

From this it becomes apparent that where expenditures associated with alternative courses of action have common elements, these can be cancelled out, because it is only the different elements of cost that are relevant to the decision.

Opportunity costs

Relevant costs are not necessarily opportunity costs, although in some circumstances they will be the same as them. An *opportunity cost* can be defined as 'the net benefit associated with using a resource in its next best alternative use'.

The *Penguin Dictionary of Economics* by G. Bannock, R.E. Baxter and R. Rees, has the following to say: 'Opportunity cost: In economics, it is considered appropriate to define cost in terms of the value of the alternatives or other opportunities which have to be forgone in order to achieve a particular thing ... opportunity cost is concerned with the real sacrifice involved in achieving something.'

It is when the opportunity cost associated with a resource is different for some of the possible pathways being examined in a particular decision analysis that it becomes a relevant cost. Opportunity costs can be divided into external and internal ones.

External opportunity costs are: 'The difference between the total net cash flows as measured between those arising from the acceptance of an opportunity as compared to its rejection.' Normally the external opportunity cost will be the buying price of a commodity or resource; however, this is not always the case.

Internal opportunity costs are: 'The net benefit associated with accepting the best alternative opportunity.' Thus it concerns the value of the second-best opportunity. From this it can be seen that the internal opportunity cost concept will apply to two situations. One is where the use of a scarce resource is being considered. In such situations the internal opportunity cost reflects scarcity. The other is when the opportunities being considered concern the mutually exclusive use of a resource, that is where, if a decision was made to use the resource for one purpose, it would preclude using that resource for some other purpose. For example, agricultural land taken for building purposes could not be farmed again until the buildings were demolished and the land 're-claimed'.

Problems of counting and measuring

There are problems associated with the production of information which is countable and measurable. The question of the homogeneity of the items being measured has to be brought into the analysis. For example, how similar are goods in a product range being made by a consumer-durable manufacturer? Television sets, for example, have many different screen sizes and may be black and white or colour. There may be occasions when it will be appropriate to 'count' the production by adding together all the TV sets produced by a manufacturer in a period, and to state that so many physical units have been produced. Sometimes global information on the number of sets produced may be of use – rather than being merely interesting. When this is done it is important to remember that such a count does not concern homogeneous items and is not very helpful as far as ascertaining such things as the average cost of producing each of the diverse models or the average revenues obtained from selling them. Nor is it useful for decision-making purposes.

As far as decision-making is concerned, a measure which will convert information about heterogeneous items, such as that concerning production costs, to a homogeneous basis is usually required. The measure most frequently used for this purpose is money. However, even a money measure does not always overcome all the problems associated with the measurement of items in the management information field. Even if inflation is assumed away, other problems associated with the use of money as a measure remain.

Another major problem stems from the use of the accruals concept which concerns the matching of costs and expenses to the revenues that they help generate. This requires the apportionment of any indirect costs associated with the joint production of goods, or where the production of goods takes place over more than one accounting period. Although some reasonable method of allocating indirect costs to products or to periods has frequently to be considered, the contribution approach is often more relevant. Nevertheless, even when the contribution approach is used, information about indirect costs may still have to be provided so that there is a complete picture of what is involved.

Measurement problems are also often complicated by the fact that different types of information will be required for different purposes. For example, when trying to ascertain for recording purposes what is the 'full cost' of manufacturing a product, all the costs associated with its production will have to be listed, and to enable this to be done some apportionment of indirect costs will need to be made – whereas for decision purposes only the costs relevant to the decision on hand should be considered, and in this sunk or fixed costs may not be at all relevant.

However, rather than completely omitting information which is irrelevant to the person using it, it can often be more beneficial to present a complete picture of the situation in a way which will highlight the various categories of information involved for different uses. Otherwise information users may feel that some things have been overlooked in the original synthesis and analysis of the decision data. For example, a decision-maker who receives only relevant information may feel that some things have been overlooked and so try to incorporate these into the analysis himself – when in fact, this had already been done.

Qualitative information

The foregoing discussion has been couched in terms of quantitative rather than qualitative factors. *Quantitative information* is 'that information which can be expressed objectively in terms of figures'. *Qualitative information* is 'information which requires subjective evaluation because it is not initially in terms of numbers'.

If qualitative factors are important to a particular decision analysis these must not be ignored. However, decisions are generally made solely using data about the factors involved which can be quantified – for example, using the costs of the possible alternative courses of action which can be verified by transactions in the market, usually on a historic cost basis. Nevertheless, there may be important considerations raised during the decision-making process by qualitative information. Yet qualitative factors are frequently ignored, either because any attempt to translate them into money terms is likely to provide an imprecise result or because they may be impossible to measure.

Nevertheless, in some cases it will be relatively easy to quantify qualitative factors – for example, where the cost of obtaining the same quality of service can be observed in the market, such as through the hiring of a resource. This would be the situation where a person has a choice between taking a bus or a taxi ride for the same journey. The difference between the prices of using these two forms of transport can be considered as the cost of the qualitative factors associated with the two forms of transport – such as convenience, speed and comfort.

Commercial and industrial undertakings frequently face making decisions where the qualitative factors influence preference when the final choice is made. However, these are frequently brought in in a subjective way – if not ignored. For example, where the price of a ticket at two cinemas showing different films is the same and a person decides to go and see one film in preference to the other, the qualitative factors concerning the storyline, the stars, the director, and so on will have been implicitly quantified, even if in a subjective way by the person choosing which film they will see.

Then, when the contribution approach is used in a make or buy decision, any qualitative factors involved are generally left out of the analysis. Rarely is it suggested that if short-run spare capacity becomes available and is to be used to make some item, rather than buying in the part, the cost of eventually returning to an original supplier needs to be incorporated into the appraisal. However, the qualitative costs associated with becoming self-reliant should be added to the other more easily verifiable costs when the firm is considering whether it should make the products itself in future.

A simple example of the approach of quantifying qualitative factors can be seen by looking at the manpower and materials factors of production. It may cost a firm less to employ an inexperienced production controller, but the work of such a person is likely to be inferior to that of an experienced counterpart. This fact is likely to be highlighted by adverse labour efficiency or material usage variances. In a case such as this the organisational decision-maker must try to impute some value to qualitative factors in the analysis of the alternatives in terms of losses in production or the wastage of materials which are likely to occur through using lower-quality employees. Another example is where the use of cheaper materials or components would reduce the cost of making a product, but also reduce its quality. An attempt must be made to answer the question of how customers are likely to react to a lower-quality product.

It is well known that the effect of a decision to substitute factors of production of a different quality when manufacturing a product may show up in terms of such things as lost custom, larger numbers of rejects, more complaints, or greater servicing costs, all arising at later dates. Such factors as these are likely to affect the future of the firm's goodwill and profits. So decision-makers must try to quantify any qualitative factors associated with a decision that they are about to make, and at the very least consider this information informally.

Quantifying qualitative information
Although it may be that the qualitative factors are weighed implicitly by the decision-maker, the more that he tries to put an explicit value on them in money terms the better it will be. For even when this cannot be done precisely, the very fact that an effort is being made to do this must ultimately lead to better decisions, because there will have been more thought behind them. Therefore the decision-maker must try to translate that information, which is not initially measurable, into quantitative terms, that is, an attempt must be made to try to bring any qualitative information available into the analysis by quantifying it.

Obviously this presents difficulties. At first sight some things appear to be impossible to measure. Nevertheless, where there is information available which has no obvious measuring device associated with it, an attempt must be made to impute quantitative value to qualitative factors. This could be done by developing a points and weighting system.

In the act of quantifying the qualitative information, management must inevitably become involved in its complexities. It is only by the careful collection and consideration of qualitative as well as quantitative information that people can hope to improve the quality of decisions made within their organisation.

It is extremely important to remember that there are costs associated with collecting, processing and interpreting information. These costs will frequently be higher as far as qualitative information is concerned. So additional amounts of information collected to help make a particular decision are eventually likely to suffer from diminishing returns. There is also the point that obtaining increasing volumes, and a better quality of information, usually adds to the time and cost associated with collecting and analysing it. Therefore sometimes less perfect information obtained quickly and cheaply will be more appropriate and of more value in the decision-making process than information of a better quality which cost a lot but arrived too late. This 'timeliness' in information gathering and analysis can be important and should not be overlooked. If a report is not produced on time its value may be reduced, and the time and effort put into the collection and compilation of the information may well have been wasted.

REFERENCES

- Argyris, C (1952), *The Impact of Budgets on People*, New York, Ithaca.
- Ashton, D, Hopper, T and Scapens, R W (eds) (1991), *Issues in Management Accounting*, Prentice-Hall.
- Becker, S, and Green, D (1962), 'Budgeting and Employee Behaviour', *The Journal of Business*, October, pp 392–402.
- Chow, C W (1983), 'The Effects of Job Standards, Tightness and Compensation Schemes on Performance: An Exploration of Linkages', *The Accounting Review*, pp 667–685.
- Crockett, F, (1992), 'Revitalising Executive Information Systems', *Sloan Management Review*, Summer.
- Cyert, R M, and March, J G (1963), *A Behavioural Theory of the Firm*, Prentice-Hall.
- Emmanuel, C, Otley, D and Merchant, K (1990), *Accounting for Management Control*, Chapman & Hall, 2nd edition .
- Ezzamel, M and Hart, H (1987), *Advanced Management Accounting: An Organisational Emphasis*, Cassell.
- Fitzgerald, L, Johnston, R, Brignall, S, Silvestro, R and Voss, C (1991), *Performance Measurement in Service Businesses*, CIMA.
- Fitzgerald, L and Moon P (1996), *Performance Measurement in Service Industries: Making It Work*, CIMA.
- Govindarajan, V (1984), 'Appropriateness of accounting data in performance evaluation: an empirical evaluation of environmental uncertainty as an intervening variable', *Accounting, Organisations and Society*, 2, pp 125–135.
- Hilton, R W (1994), *Managerial Accounting*, McGraw-Hill.
- Hofstede, G H (1968), *The Game of Budget Control*, Tavistock.
- Hopwood, A (1972), 'An empirical study of the role of accounting data in performance evaluation', *Journal of Accounting Research* (supplement), 10, pp 156–182.
- Kaplan, R S and Norton D P (1992), 'The balanced scorecard – measures that drive performance', *Harvard Business Review*, January – February, pp 71–79.
- Kenis, I (1979), 'Effects of budgetary goal characteristics on managerial attitudes and

performance', *The Accounting Review*, 54, pp 707–721.

- Lynch R L and Cross, K F (1991), *Measure up! Yardsticks for continuous improvements*, Blackwell.
- Merchant, K A (1987), 'How and why firms disregard the controllability problem', in Burns and Kaplan (eds), *Accounting and Management Field Study Perspectives*, Harvard Business School Press .
- Moizer, P (1991), 'Performance Appraisal and Rewards', in Ashton et al., *Issues in Management Accounting*.
- Otley, D (1987), *Accounting control and organisational behaviour*, Heinemann.
- Otley, D (1990) 'Issues in accountability and control: some observations from a study of colliery accountability in the British Coal Corporation', *Management Accounting Research*, June, pp 101–123.
- Simmonds, K (1981) 'Strategic management accounting', *Management Accounting*, (ICMA), April, pp 26–29.
- Tosi, H (1975) 'The human effects of managerial budgeting systems', in Livingstone, J. (ed.), *Management Accounting: The Behavioural Foundations*, Grid Columbus, Ohio.

Chapter 5

The Communication of Information

'Effective control clearly depends on the existence of appropriate information systems, and the application of information technology, has the potential to improve the control systems' (Harvey, 1994). He makes a number of valuable, appropriate general points concerning the communication of information:

THE COMMUNICATION OF INFORMATION

Michael Harvey, 'Balancing Facts against Figures' (part), *Certified Accountant*, July 1984

The way in which information is communicated is also important. Although high-quality information may have been collected, if it is badly presented to the decision-taker it may be misunderstood, poorly assimilated, or at the extreme completely ignored. Therefore, there are a number of principles of communication that the information gatherer must be aware of. First, it is essential to find out *why* the information is required, and then *whom* it is for. This will enable a decision to be made as to *what* information should be produced and *when*, as well as *how* it should be presented. For example, if the information is of a financial nature and is to be used by a non-financial manager, the level of the recipient's financial and accounting knowledge and competence must be ascertained before deciding what information to provide and how to present it. Therefore, jargon that is unlikely to be understood by the recipient must be avoided, or an education programme must be initiated to explain the technicalities of the information to its potential users. The level of the recipient's ability to grasp and analyse situations also needs to be taken into account. The workload of the people to whom the information is to be supplied must also be considered. This is particularly important in order to avoid reports which are too detailed going to busy people who will then use them inappropriately – if they use them at all.

This all means that a discussion with the eventual recipient of the information should take place to ascertain for what purpose the information is required, and how best it could be presented to help its eventual user. For example, questions should be asked about whether the information is of a routine nature, or for a special situation, and how soon it is required.

The collector and the producer of the information must decide on such things as how the report should be presented and consider its timely production as far as the decision-maker is concerned. In some cases where information is required to help people make regular minor decisions, such as when used for control purposes, it should be possible to design a suitable form for both the collection and the reporting of the information. In other cases, such as where *ad hoc* information is required to help in the analysis of an important decision, careful consideration must be given to the form and presentation of the report. In such situations it is normal to highlight the conclusions and the recommendations in précis form and so help a busy recipient, with any supporting information and details of the sources of references being provided as an appendix to enable the reader to follow these up as wished. Care must be taken in the method used to present statistical information. It may be appropriate to provide this in tabular, graphical or diagrammatical form, if this will help in its understanding and assimilation.

In all this, remember the *cost* of collecting, analysing and presenting the information.

Frequently the conventional methods of producing even objective data, such as through the use of cost accounting records, can deal with only certain aspects of the information, and even then this will sometimes be in an arbitrary manner. For generally this will be based on historical cost accounting systems, and so will not highlight the relevant aspects of the information that the decision-maker needs to isolate. Another deficiency is that such records rarely provide environmental information.

This all means that the producer of information for decision-making purposes must ensure that the decision-taker is made familiar with relevant cost and opportunity cost concepts. He must also help the decision-taker to become more sophisticated in the analysis of the information that is being provided, by not including common data, only information which differs from one possible alternative decision pathway to another – but explaining what has been done.

Finally, the people supplying information to decision-makers must be aware of the difficulties of measurement and counting as far as some aspects of information they are providing are concerned. They must also attempt to improve methods of quantifying any qualitative information relevant to the decision.

In the article already quoted in part in Chapter 4, Crockett also stresses the need for a high-quality executive information system.

REVITALISING EXECUTIVE INFORMATION SYSTEMS (part)
F Crockett, *Sloan Management Review*, Summer 1992

In *Scale and Scope*, Alfred Chandler argues that outstanding US companies in the 1920s and 1930s, like DuPont, were successful in large part because they devised innovative information systems. In contrast, he argues, the more diversified companies of the 1970s were not as successful because top managers 'had to rely on impersonal statistical data that had become far less relevant.... The overload resulted, not from any lack of information, but from its lack of quality and from the senior decision-maker's lack of ability to evaluate it.'

During the 1980s, many executives tried to get higher-quality information by buying and installing executive information systems (EISs) or executive support systems (ESSs). An EIS has been defined as a 'computerised system that provides executives with easy access to internal and external information that is relevant to their critical success factors'. I would change this definition slightly. An EIS does not need to be fully computerised; I have developed systems with clients that have some manual interfaces because the cost of automating data extraction and combination from multiple databases has been too high. Also, I would emphasise the system's ability to facilitate the highest levels of strategic decision-making. An EIS can be constructed to help diagnose problems and develop solutions.

Figure 1: Benefits of an executive information system

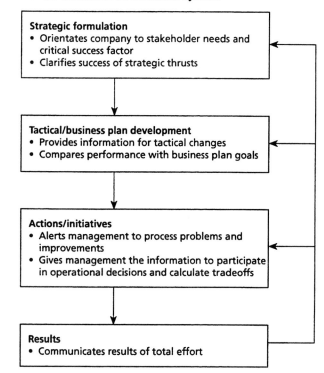

Figure 1 shows the benefits of an EIS. Performance results provide feedback that influence (1) strategy formulation, by focusing executives on stakeholder needs and the critical success factors, (2) business plan development, by providing information on changes and monitoring progress, and (3) operational activities, by alerting executives to problem areas and improvements.

Although research has documented isolated instances of EIS success – at companies such as Xerox, Phillips Petroleum, Boeing, Firestone, Gillette, and Lincoln National – the larger corporate market has not embraced EISs. Installers have estimated that the US market reached only $60 million in 1989, and some experts believe that half of the systems set up in the 1980s have failed to provide real advantage to their purchasers.

Most researchers have blamed these problems on technical difficulties or on senior executives' reluctance to use computers. Based on my work with clients in Price Waterhouse's Strategic Consulting Group, I believe these two problems may be less significant than they once were. Most technical problems with EISs have been, or are in the process of being, resolved and senior executives are becoming more eager to try anything that might help them solve complex problems.

My experience has been that the primary problem with EISs is that the *right* information is not reaching senior executives. Working with clients and drawing from the existing literature, I have developed a methodology to increase the quality of information flowing into EISs. In this paper, I will describe three primary problems that retard the flow of quality information into EISs and a four-step process for solving these problems. Throughout, I illustrate these ideas with examples from client experiences.

These are the three basic information problems that plague EIS use:

- Systems still do not provide (or provide too late) the data that senior managers consider crucial, even after installation.
- Collected data are not linked across functions or strategic areas.
- The data that are available help diagnose problems but do not help find solutions.

Lack of crucial data

EISs were originally developed to provide executives with crucial data, yet they have not done so. One of my clients decided that a critical success factor was development of a low-cost design and manufacturing process in order to become the low-cost producer. However, the client had no way to aggregate its cost data along product lines. An EIS was developed in part to deal with this problem. Two years into the project, however, little progress has been made toward collecting this vital information. Design and manufacturing costs remained separate; they were not linked to allow executives to analyse the product portfolio.

Researchers have located part of the problem in system development. Often system architects are technically competent but not sufficiently knowledgeable about business. They emphasise the technology over the information going into it, as if all information were equally important. The company's changing strategic goals seem to have no impact on the system. Executives in one of my client companies complained about the tendency of their technicians to care most about how well the system functioned and least about the information. When these executives decided to change the way they viewed their target market and focus on different variables, this problem became especially acute. After six months, senior managers tried to find out whether their more focused marketing efforts had improved sales to the target market, only to learn that the existing databases could not distinguish sales to this segment from overall sales information.

Middle managers who collect the data also contribute to the problem. It is often against their own interests to change data collection. In many cases, they do not understand how strategic changes affect their efforts. I've seen this happen many times. In a manufacturing company, senior executives issued a new strategy, but middle managers responsible for finding the information continued to collect data based on its availability rather than its relevancy to the new strategy.

Linkage problems

Difficulties in linking data across functions are often behind some of the more intractable technical problems of EISs but when these difficulties are solved, the usefulness of EISs is significantly increased. In one of my client companies, functional departments had numerous databases containing important strategic information, but the information was not distributed outside the departments until it was too late to make a difference.

The linkages should be organised around business issues that are crucial to carrying out the strategy. For example, a company had identified market share as a primary strategic issue. The EIS project team linked sales data (volume projections of existing products) and product development data (expected timing of new product introductions) to show executives at a glance the impact this data made on market share. The data was presented not as isolated, descriptive numbers but as part of a prescriptive response to a critical business issue.

Lack of problem-solving

Many CEOs complain that they know more about their companies' problems than they want to know – what they need are solutions. One company had an elaborate EIS that kept showing that sales decreases over several years were directly linked to customer perceptions of declining quality. But the system did not tell them how to attack quality problems.

EISs *can* be programmed to help generate solutions. To do this, they must monitor the processes that often cause poor final results rather than simply the results themselves. Instead of focusing on one strategic decision and the information necessary to make it, systems should monitor key processes over time. For example, in a company that sets a goal of increasing annual new product introductions, the EIS can monitor progress by revealing ongoing market research findings and ongoing research and development investments. The EIS becomes an early warning system rather than a conveyor of yearly results.

For another example, a company that is implementing a program to improve worker safety could evaluate the program by looking at the total number of lost-time accidents at each plant. But this information does not show *why* the initiative is working or not. A process-oriented system would look at data such as the number of people trained in the safety program, the investment in safety-related facility improvements, and the percentage of plants passing internal safety inspections.

Managers often do not distinguish between process information and results information. Overlooking process information, they miss solutions. The senior executives at the company with sales decreases described above were aware of the poor results but could not fathom their precise source.

Improving EISs

EISs can be more useful if companies take a multiphased approach that co-ordinates strategic, operational, and organisational demands. The key element is the linkage among stakeholder expectations, critical success factors, and performance measures. Stakeholders include a company's stockholders, suppliers, regulators, customers, employees, and so forth. It takes a great deal of primary and secondary research to precisely understand stakeholder expectations. I have noticed, however, that even when executives review stakeholder information, they do it only sporadically. Moreover, such data often are not continually updated or regularly compared against data flowing from internal operational functions. I have found that only when a system is designed around performance measurements that give expectations of stakeholders the same weight and value as critical success factors and their benchmarks does the system help improve strategic decision-making.

In order to devise such a system, the company must identify and determine the correct performance measures for critical success factors and stakeholder expectations. These performance measures help executives determine the success or failure of activities. Performance measures are the foundation of a useful EIS.

The dynamic nature of business creates an additional problem for developing EISs. I believe that EISs have not performed as well as expected partly because industries have changed so much in the last fifteen years. A system must be able to respond to strategic changes and new critical success factors. In principle, executives should review the components of the system as often as they revise their strategic initiatives. However, revising information needs and adapting the system can be costly. Researchers have suggested an 80/20 approach that appears to offer the major benefits of strategic data planning and targeting approaches. While the specific aspects of the 80/20 approach vary among individual firms, the basic aim is to 'zero in quickly on the key "products" to be implemented (bottom up), while reducing the amount of effort spent on global planning (top down)'.

Some of my clients have decreased costs by changing their data requirements only when they achieve a consensus that the change is necessary. They require multiple sign-off procedures among managers before costly changes are made. In one company, a manager who wanted a critical change had to make a detailed proposal that included the strategic rationale. A cross-section of executives reviewed such proposals. Approved changes were made in batches periodically to reduce disruptions.

A good example of a strategy change that will affect an EIS is institution of a just-in-time (JIT) manufacturing system. A company that initiates JIT does not need to focus as much on labour efficiency as it has in the past. Unless it changes its EIS to monitor variables such as manufacturing flexibility and responsiveness, it will not know whether it is meeting its JIT goals.

[With regard to reporting information, Crockett continues:]

- **Step three: Determine reporting formats and frequency.** For EISs to be successful, executives must receive the right quality of information in an understandable form, both on the computer screen and as hard copy. They must also be able to customise the way the information is viewed. At the soft-goods manufacturer [see p.59], for example, the detail-oriented CEO personally edited the financial information by eliminating the bar graphs and creating tables of figures.

The project team develops an appropriate format – tables, graphs, or text – for each performance measure. Then, the team uses a question methodology to establish the links between the data and strategic issues. Figure 3 shows how the Fortune 100 company did this. This sequence of questions guides presentation of the data.

Figure 3: Sample of question methodology

Overall strategy	How does company A attain a low-cost, high quality manufacturing effort?		
Broad critical success factors	Are design efforts being simplified?	Are manufacturing initiatives being implemented?	Are service efforts being improved?
Specific critical success factors	Are synchronous efforts being adopted?	Are quality levels improving?	Is scheduling more efficient?
Measure results	• Number of inventory returns • Percentage of capacity utilisation • Percentage of workers cross-trained	• Number of defects • — • —	• Plant hours scheduled • — • —

Figure 4 shows how I structured a report for a high-tech components manufacturer with a 'straw man' approach. Each chapter concerned a key business issue and included cross-functional performance measures tied to critical success factors and stakeholder expectations. For instance, the chapter on cost containment included a graph showing how product design complexity affected cost (see Figure 5). The report also included manageable tables of numbers. These first 'straw man' reports or mock-ups contain illustrative data, showing the report formats and logical sequence.

The executives who will be receiving EIS reports should review the formats ahead of time and offer suggestions. They will often notice gaps. In a Fortune 500 company, the senior vice-president of marketing noticed a lack of information about his distribution channel support efforts. Team members went back to identify and define relevant measures, such as broker satisfaction. Watson et al. have found that 92 per cent of the companies they studied used an iterative prototyping methodology.

An executive may also find that the level of detail is overwhelming and unhelpful and may ask that the reports be simplified. For the most part, however, I have found that executives are amazed by these reports. In the Fortune 500 company, it was only after senior managers reviewed the straw man reports that they felt the project team was making any tangible progress. Until that point, they deemed the whole project nice in theory but impossible to implement.

- **Step four: Outline information flows and how information can be used.** In this step, the organisation decides on the precise method of data collection, the timing of collection, and the process of generating the reports. The result is a data flow diagram showing the path of the data from source to executives. One company assigned employees to monitor specific measures and appointed a data co-ordinator to ensure the integrity of the data, the timeliness of the reports, and delivery to the appropriate executives.

    The organisation also needs to establish processes that will encourage use of the information. I generally advocate a series of regular manager and employee meetings for review of specific reports or subsets of information. Senior executives use the information to reinforce initiatives, reward behaviour, and change strategies. Employees learn how to adjust operations and respond to strategic needs.

    In the Fortune 100 company, the project team helped management determine the sequence of meetings in which EIS information would be used. For example, the sales department decided to meet regularly with the plant manager and his scheduler to improve order entry procedures and thus, speed up deliveries to the distribution channel. The EIS gave senior executives the information to monitor and guide employee decisions and to watch *longitudinal progress.*

Figure 4: Sample report

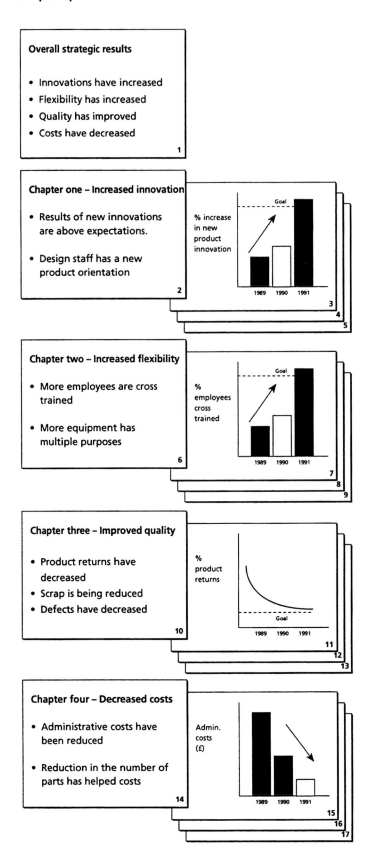

Figure 5: Sample illustration from EIS report

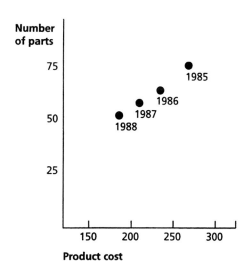

Realising EIS potential

Quality information is critical to decision-making. But even true believers in the power of EISs are not receiving the kind of quality information they expected. At least half the systems are not living up to expectations. The senior managers who are supposed to be using EISs are ignoring them.

It turns out that the hardware and software are not the problem – the information or data going into the system is. For companies that installed executive information or support systems in the 1980s, this methodology can help recoup their investment and revitalise the decision-making process. For companies considering installation of such a system, following these four steps can decrease development costs and increase the system's effectiveness. Either way, senior managers' expectations regarding EISs can be fulfilled, and their strategic decision-making can be enhanced.

SUMMARY AND IMPLICATIONS FOR MANAGEMENT ACCOUNTANTS

During the 1970s some of the data presented to managers was either irrelevant or the managers lacked the ability to evaluate it properly. In the 1980s managers tried to get higher-quality information by buying and installing EISs. Still the right information was not sifting through. Crockett's main emphasis in this article is to identify the reasons behind this failure.

There are three problems that hamper the flow of appropriate information.

- Systems still do not provide/provide too late the data that senior managers consider crucial.
- Collected data are not linked across functions or strategic areas.
- Available data help diagnose problems but do not help find solutions.

Crockett then presents a four-step module for solving these problems. To ensure that the right strategic information flows into its EIS, a company should:

- Identify the critical success factors and stakeholder expectations.
- Document performance measures that monitor them.
- Determine the EIS reporting formats and frequency.
- Outline information flows and how the information can be used.

Quality information is critical to decision-making but EIS systems are still not living up to expectations. The information that is going into the system is the problem. Management accountants need to reconsider the relevance and usefulness of the data going into the system and how it can best be used to aid strategic business decisions.

The success of Japanese manufacturing firms has resulted in considerable attention being paid to their methods of management in general, and approaches to financial control and performance evaluation in particular.

Chapter 6

Concluding Observations

It is quite probable that a newly designed performance management system will be introduced to replace an existing set of possibly piecemeal measures. The CMA Guideline (*ibid.*) offers a number of observations for dealing with this situation; it also points out the system's dynamic nature and stresses the need for top management support to ensure successful implementation and operation, as the following extracts show.

RE-EVALUATING PERFORMANCE EVALUATION AND THE REWARD SYSTEM
Society of Management Accountants of Canada, Management Accounting Guideline 31,
***Developing Comprehensive Performance Indicators,* 1994**

If a firm has established a set of goals, strategies, and objectives, and then developed performance indicators that focus on the critical success factors for the firm, the firm's performance evaluation and reward system must be re-evaluated to assure that it is consistent with the new performance indicators. If not, managers will continue to be motivated by an old system that is not consistent with the new one.

For example, if customer service, quality, and speed are critical, and performance indicators are developed to support them, but if a manager is not rewarded in some way for quality and speed of performance, there is a great likelihood that the manager will behave inconsistently with the goals, strategies, and objectives of the firm. The manager may respond in a way absolutely antithetical to that desired.

Many firms, although espousing an emphasis on customer service, quality, speed, new product development, product variety, and value to their customers, still have not introduced performance evaluation and reward systems that are consistent with these thrusts. It could also be said that what managers actually do is very different. Examples would include mail-order houses that make customers wait for a number of telephone rings before answering their call; supermarkets that make customers wait in check-out lines for long periods of time; and automobile dealership service departments that treat customers as though they are not interested in their business.

It has been said that a firm 'gets what is measured'. A firm gets a lot of things, many of them bad, in the name of achieving the things that are measured. For example, quality may suffer when people try to meet a schedule. It could also be said that a firm 'doesn't get what is not measured'. It behooves many firms to reconsider and realign their performance reward systems to be consistent with their performance indicator practices.

ENSURING CONTINUAL IMPROVEMENT

A new performance indicator system is just that – new – and probably will need to be adjusted after it has been put in place and is found to satisfy some aspects of management's needs but not others. New indicators may have to be added and others dropped.

The frequency with which information is provided may have to be altered. In time, the performance indicator system will coincide with the firm's goals, strategies, and objectives; will focus on critical success factors; and will provide information to assist managers in their decision-making process in an attempt to increase stakeholder value.

However, tomorrow's business environment probably will be as different from today's as today's is from yesterday's. Just as yesterday's approaches to performance measurement are inadequate and have to be changed, so, too, firms can expect to continually need to update as they move forward into the twenty-first century. As the external environment changes, what's important and unimportant within the firm also changes, and new indicators must be introduced and old ones eliminated.

ENSURING TOP MANAGEMENT SUPPORT AND COMMITMENT

Because management may be very familiar and comfortable with deeply entrenched performance measurement systems, there may be significant reservations about change. Others in the organisation will also be familiar with existing practices; although they may not feel as comfortable with the specific measures, they understand that those are the measures by which they will be evaluated. As a result, they respond accordingly, even though utilising a different measurement system could prompt different responses.

Senior management commitment and support for new performance indicators that are significantly different from current practice can be obtained in several ways.

Senior management may clearly see the changes that are taking place in their business environment, fully appreciate what it requires to be successful, and initiate steps that cause the organisation to focus and track new critical success factors. Xerox, for example, during the 1970s lost considerable market share to a number of Japanese copier manufacturers. The company realised that their quality, new-product development cycle time, and product costs, no longer successfully competed. Xerox actually discovered that their Japanese competitors were making a profit with a selling price almost equal to Xerox's unit manufacturing cost. Heightened emphasis on quality, new-product development cycle time, and low cost has enabled Xerox to recover much of its lost market share.

Harley-Davidson found itself in a similar situation during the late 1970s and early 1980s. Their motorcycles lacked Japanese quality and reliability. Costs had risen significantly in a ten-year period. Increased emphasis on quality, just-in-time manufacturing, and cost management has resulted in the company regaining its lost market position.

Some companies have demonstrated an ability to visualise longer term, see impending threats approaching and take the necessary proactive steps to protect against them. In the early 1980s, General Electric saw global competition becoming stronger and clearly stated that they must be number one or number two in every business category in which they were involved or they would disengage. This prompted much more focus on customer requirements, competitive strengths and weaknesses, and GE's own internal capabilities. Some businesses have been dropped and others added. A host of new performance indicators have been introduced dealing with quality, particularly fast response, and productivity.

There have been some examples where business units, rather than the corporation as a whole, have had enough independence to think through their own business situation, recognise the changing nature of it and of the factors that determine success, and establish a new set of performance indicators that have improved that unit's performance. This local example has become an internal benchmark for other parts and, ultimately, for the firm as a whole.

Whatever the impetus for new comprehensive performance indicators, it is essential that, in time, they have the full commitment of the senior-most management if they are going to help sustain competitiveness in the changing business environment. Utimately, the new performance indicator system must be used to manage the business.

Top management can demonstrate its support and commitment by actively leading the new performance indicators initiative or making it the mainstay of their focus and impetus. Robert Galvin, former CEO of Motorola, was the friving force for that company's heightened emphasis on quality through its 'Six Sigma' quality standard. David Kearn's emphasis on quality at Xerox, John Young's emphasis on speed at Hewlett-Packard, and Jack Welch's emphasis on speed, simplicity, and candor at GE are further examples.

Top management leadership, involvement in steering committees, constant emphasis on the new factors, and support for the development and refinement of a new performance indicator system are essential if such a system is going to be developed, introduced, and improved, and if it is to be effective.

Finally, Harvey (1994) also comments on the need for managerial involvement, and additionally, employees at all levels in an organisation.

STRATEGIC PLANNING IN PRACTICE
Michael Harvey, *Strategic Management Accountancy and Marketing: Practical Elements*, CIMA 1994

When an economy thrives all but inept businesses survive – sometimes in spite of their management! However, it is during favourable economic conditions that a firm must take the opportunity to develop its corporate strategy. By doing so it can operate in survival mode when an economic downturn inevitably arrives.

Enterprises operating a system of corporate planning must involve top management in the process. They must ensure that there are consistent strategies over time. The process should systematically seek out growth areas and new business opportunities but also develop contingency plans to deal with possible environmental changes, whether these be favourable or unfavourable. For example, when an election is imminent and where a change of government would affect operations, the firm must develop contingency plans to cope with the likely policies of whichever party gains power. For an entity to come out of a downturn in the economy successfully it is important to harness the potential of all levels of its employees. John Argenti's definition of corporate planning clearly highlights the importance of middle management in the process when he states that a corporate plan can be described as 'a set of instructions to the managers of an organisation describing what role each constituent part is expected to play in the achievement of the organisation's corporate objectives'. Tom Peters and Robert Waterman go even further by pointing out the importance of the lowest level of employee when they state: 'one of the main clues to corporate excellence [comes from] unusual effort on the part of apparently ordinary employees'.